THE GOVERNOR'S CHESSBOARD

A LIFETIME OF PUBLIC POLICY

RICHARD D. LAMM

Library of Congress Control Number: 2019946403

ISBN 978-1-68275-249-4

Printed in the United States of America.
0 9 8 7 6 5 4 3 2 1

Fulcrum Publishing
4690 Table Mountain Drive, Suite 100
Golden, Colorado 80403
800-992-2908 • 303-277-1623
fulcrumbookstore.ipgbook.com

CONTENTS

PREFACE

On January 7, 1975, I walked out the west entrance of the Colorado State Capitol to be inaugurated Colorado's thirty-eighth governor. It was a brisk but sunny winter day and a crowd of about one thousand people were assembled there to see and hear the state officers sworn in. I was thirty-nine years old and had never run anything larger than a two-person law firm. I had already appointed most of my cabinet, and I was apprehensive because I had to make a significant speech, but overall I was confident. The nation had just endured the nightmare of Watergate and the press was in an investigative mood. Colorado politics were growing ever meaner. There were already bumper stickers that read: "Lamm Walked the State, but Cannot Run It." My journey was long and exciting. I had passionate friends and passionate enemies. Looking back on it, I am not sure I should have been that confident. I had accumulated my fair share of life experiences, but...

I had risen rapidly in the Colorado political system. From the first days of my Colorado political career, I had challenged the status quo and the assumed wisdom. I came to the state permanently in November of 1961 not knowing a soul, and a year later I was president of the Denver Young Democrats. Five years later I was elected to the Colorado legislature, six years later I was elected assistant minority leader, and thirteen years later I was elected governor. In the process, I had authored and shepherded through the legislature the nation's first liberalized abortion bill and led the successful campaign against hosting the 1976 Winter Olympics in Colorado. Conventional wisdom on both these issues at the time I raised them was that I was committing "political suicide."

I was not a natural politician. My primary education was during World War II in a one-room schoolhouse. A move to Pittsburgh, Pennsylvania, in the middle of sixth grade made me shy and left me feeling inadequate among students in my new, sophisticated, upper-middle-class suburban school. I loved my previous years in that small classroom, where there were approximately thirty students from first to sixth grade, and I loved the lifestyle of our semirural community. I could swim, fish, and hunt, but I knew nothing of popular music, film, or the post–World War II lifestyle. This was pre-television, and I did not have the unifying force of a national culture portrayed by the new TV shows and magazines. I was a rural boy from a farm community, and I didn't share any of my new fellow students' interests. I was way behind in the curriculum, and I often didn't feel up to the level of instruction. It took me a long time to make friends, and I was well into my high school years before I felt comfortable and accepted. My friends in high school were underachievers who knew a lot about cars but little else. One teacher called us a bunch of "laggers," which we considered a compliment, adopting it as the name of our clique. I loved those friends and am in contact with them to this day, but they were not role models for much of my latter life.

This was not the clay to mold a politician. I was never active in school politics or events and could not come close to distinguishing between Republicans and Democrats. By college my social status was dramatically improved, but I had to work to offset college expenses and took absolutely no role in any campus organizations.

My "Road to Damascus" moment was when John F. Kennedy ran for president. Shazam! as the comic book character said to turn himself into a superhero. The example and the charisma of John F. Kennedy captivated me and clearly inspired my interest in politics. It was in my second year of law school—late by the standards of many of my contemporaries—but the change in my politics and my interest in public policy came almost like a religious conversion. I suddenly saw the light.

But an even more influential part of my political philosophy came when I was a fifth grader in that one-room schoolhouse. It was during this time when math took us into exponential growth, and I was able to see the impact of compounding. It is interesting that of all the hours I spent in class those six years, our teacher's explanation of compound growth stays with me to this day and has had a profound influence on my thinking.

A significant part of my life flowed from Mrs. Reed, my teacher in that one-room school in northern Illinois, where I spent first grade to the middle of my sixth-grade year. It may sound insignificant given all the myriad influences that affect a child during the first twelve years, but I remember it vividly to this day. Mrs. Reed told of the bet between the Sultan and the Jester in which the Sultan asked what the stakes of the bet were. The jester said, "Very modest, Sire, just place one grain of rice on the first square of the chessboard, then double on the second square and double it for each square on the chessboard." It sounds so modest, but the kicker is that there is not enough rice in the kingdom to pay such stakes! Most people don't understand how rapidly geometric growth explodes. Thirty lineal steps take you thirty feet away, thirty exponential steps take you twice around the world.

I was controversial. I had already fought some major political battles, and I have always been a bit of a political heretic. It served me well—until it didn't. Getting involved in controversial issues set me apart from the crowd and contributed to my success… and failure. I am to this day regarded with suspicion by large parts of the Democratic Party. Rather than a team player, I have instead been more of a critic of the party. I am in politics for the ideas, not the party. I see the Democratic

Party as a special interest party, and while I am glad it is a party of compassion and generally favors the working people, it also has been captured by many special interests, including the teachers' union and the trial lawyers (to name only two). It is financed by special interest money, and while Democratic special interests are less venal than Republican interests, they are still special interests. FACT OF LIFE: Large vested interests play a dominant role in both political parties. All meaningful campaign reform of my generation has been either defeated in Congress or declared unconstitutional by the US Supreme Court. My generation has failed to do anything meaningful in campaign reform and has instead watched it get worse year after year. There are some steps that could be taken, but as long as the US Supreme Court equates money with speech, real reform is not possible. That is the reality we must live with. But how about a third political party? From experience I can say that starting a competitive third political party needs a combination of extraordinary people and extraordinary circumstances. The Republican Party was the first/last really competitive third party to form (in 1856), and it took nation-shattering circumstances (the coming Civil War) to bring it into existence. It may happen again in our lifetimes, but it is not something we can expect or count on. Almost certainly, America will have to solve its problems within the existing party structure.

The Democratic Party is still in the thrall of Keynesian economics, which I find dangerously outdated. It was the right policy for the Depression in the 1930s, but the fact that we will soon spend more to finance past consumption (the debt) than we will invest in the future is a critical reason why we must form a political coalition to accomplish the thankless task of balancing the budget and starting to pay down the debt. Democrats in the 1930s advanced Keynesian spending, and it did stimulate the economy and help America crawl out of the Depression. But both political parties missed the indispensable second part of Keynesian economics—where you pay back during good years the money you borrowed during bad years. Keynes never envisaged endless borrowing.

The Democratic Party is far stronger than the Republican Party on environmental issues but still too timid to keep us from environmental disaster. I understand, but do not excuse. I believe our society is headed for both environmental and economic disaster in the form of global warming and explosive debt. We have locked in a series of economic and environmental disasters that I believe will play out in our lifetime. Both of these problems will take the equivalent of wartime sacrifice, which is difficult or impossible in non-wartime conditions. We cannot do politically what we need to do economically to prevent large-scale trauma.

Yes, these are tough issues, and I understand why politicians are cautious. It is difficult (impossible?) for democracy to make hard choices. Democracy appears to be a crisis-activated system capable of responding to major traumas such as the crash of 1929 and Pearl Harbor in 1941, but I believe it is unable to handle creeping crises, where problems just slowly get worse day/week/year after day/week/year. We forget that two thousand years ago a number of Greek philosophers did not believe democracy was a sustainable political system. Could they be belatedly right? Democracy may work when, overall, it can give the public more and more, but can democracy work when the public is called upon to take less, to tighten their belts, to make sacrifices other than when faced with a war or equivalent trauma?

MOVE TO DENVER

I learned in November of 1961 that there were no openings at the Civil Rights Division of the Department of Justice. That same day I headed to Denver. Denver? Yes, I had already decided I wanted to live in Colorado. I had tried to have an outdoor life in California, but it was clear there was too many people and lifestyle that was too frenzied. Crossing into eastern Colorado for the third time (the first was our family vacation; the second was when I was stationed at Fort Carson). I started to think of Colorado as my long-term home. It was

November, but the weather was beautiful. Pikes Peak gradually appeared in all its magnificence. I checked into a cheap motel on Colorado Boulevard, bought the *Denver Post*, and looked at "Apartments to Rent." There were a lot of them available, but, after two days looking, none with the character I was seeking. I spent a few weary days looking for just the right place to live and just the right job.

I got a job as an accountant with Ernst and Ernst (faster than I found an apartment), one of the big eight accounting firms. I had passed the CPA exam but now needed a year of experience to actually get my certificate. The Denver office of Ernst and Ernst was a wonderful place, but ultimately I wanted to practice law, not accounting. After one year of experience doing both tax and audit work, and upon getting my certificate, I left to work for the Colorado Anti-Discrimination Commission.

Meanwhile, after my arrival in Denver and a full day of looking at prosaic apartments, I checked "Roommate Wanted" instead, and that led me to Fred Luck and 1555 Franklin Street. Fred, a mechanic in the air force working at Buckley Air Force Base, was a few years younger than I and was filled with life. The apartment was the full basement of an apartment house (torn down in the 1970s) with a gigantic living room, a study, a dining room, and one small bedroom. It had great possibilities, if you didn't mind basements. The study could easily be made into a second bedroom, and I immediately saw the potential. It helped that I liked Fred a lot.

My training as a CPA in Denver deeply affected my thinking about public policy. I believe that Roosevelt saved the nation during the Depression and that borrowed money was part of that salvation. However, beware of ideas that were appropriate to the past but can be disastrous to the future. You cannot, ultimately, build a great nation on borrowed money.

1. AN UNLIKELY POLITICIAN

SLIDING DOORS

Gwyneth Paltrow starred in a fascinating movie called *Sliding Doors*. In it, she is running to catch a subway and the doors close right in front of her. She takes the next train, and the movie takes her life in one direction. Then the movie goes back to the same scene, but this time she sticks out her hand and the doors open, she gets on, and her whole life goes in a different, and happier, direction. A haunting metaphor. I think of two sliding-door experiences in my life. The first was in November of 1961 when I moved to Denver and encountered the sliding door that allowed me to meet my future wife, Dottie.

Right after I graduated from Berkeley Law in June of 1961, and after spending the summer in San Francisco studying for the California and Colorado Bar, I decided to move to Colorado. Not precisely a sliding door but rather a carefully thought out comparison between my memories of being stationed in Colorado and the magical city of San Francisco. "Magical" it was, but three thousand people a day were moving to California.

After taking the California Bar in August (I had already flown to Colorado to take the bar there), my friend Phil Hammer decided to go to Washington, D.C., to try to get a job with the Civil Rights Division of the Department of Justice. Sounded perfect! I decided to join him. When we got there, we discovered that every other young liberal law graduate had the same idea. We were interviewed, and although we were encouraged, we were told it would be a long, uncertain wait, so I decided to go to Colorado. I do not classify this as a sliding-door experience, as it wasn't a spontaneous decision but was instead the product of months of thought and comparison. I contrast this to how I met my lovely wife, Dottie. I tremble when I think of how close we came to never having met.

I arrived in Denver in November of 1961. Soon after, my friend Jan Hess from the University of Wisconsin, who was teaching in Denver, said there was a party she'd try to get me and my roommate, Fred, invited to. It was then that the doors slid.

Jan called Dottie, one of the party's hosts, and asked if she could bring two friends. Dottie refused, as the invitation list had become unmanageable. She was sorry, and the doors were almost closed when Jan started to cry. She wanted to come to the party, but she couldn't without bringing the two of us. These were real tears because Jan was and remains sincere, honest, and guileless. Dottie, moved by the tears, finally said yes. My fate was sealed.

We arrived at the party, and there was Dottie. She was surrounded by lots of people, so I went to the phone and copied the telephone number. I knew this was a woman I badly wanted to meet. There was something about Dottie that impressed me at first glance: she was like no other woman I had ever met.

Three days later I called and invited her out for a beer. She politely said no, asking, "Which one were you?" I told her I was one of the guys Jan Hess had brought, but she still said no. I knew enough not to push too hard, so I told her I would call in exactly a week and ask again. I noted the time and exactly one week later I called again, on the exact hour I had originally called. She was impressed by this, and this time she said yes. The sliding doors opened and I waltzed right in.

I am proud to have become a politician despite the profession's low standing in the public esteem. In 1959, I was urged to support John F. Kennedy by my dear friend and law-school roommate, Phil Hammer. I had voted for Dwight D. Eisenhower in 1956, my very first vote. But to be young is to be liberal and passionate, and I was soon mesmerized by JFK. I did little for the Kennedy campaign in 1960 because, as a law student, I was studying hard to make the transfer from the University of California, Hastings, to the University of California, Boalt Hall (Berkeley). However, I was soon bitten by the political bug. And when I made the move to Denver in 1961, I immediately got involved with the Young Democrats, rising quickly to the top of the organization (no big deal—no one else wanted the job). I then got involved in Senator John Carroll's 1962 Senate campaign, which he lost to Peter Dominick.

This was a time when lots of young people were passionate about public policy. And, like me, lots of young people were attracted to JFK, politics, and the civil rights movement, and the Young Democrats grew into a large and successful organization. I was an accountant by day, but I was elected vice president of the Colorado Young Democrats in 1965 (lawyer Frank Plaut was president), and I began casting around for something meaningful to do. I soon organized a "Bury Goldwater" hootenanny with the help of my new friend Harry Tuft, who ran The Denver Folklore Center where I would retreat periodically to get relief from the pressures of my accounting job. Almost every artist, almost every musician we contacted was willing to volunteer, and we had a great event with a large and appreciative crowd. We turned the money over to the state party, and it was there that I met Dale Tooley., the chair of the Denver Democratic Party. A year and a half later, Dale came to me and encouraged me to run for the state legislature. The election was "at-large," which meant eighteen Democrats and eighteen Republicans ran for the eighteen legislative house seats allocated to Denver. At the county assembly in the summer of 1966 I received more delegate votes than any of the other newcomers. Little did I know, but I was soon to get incredibly drawn into the world of public policy and politics.

I was asked to spend a day shepherding around Hubert Humphrey, which was a real experience. What a happy campaigner! What a "Happy Warrior!" I got him back to his hotel about ten p.m., and I was wrung out and dying for the day to be over. But Senator Humphrey stood in the hotel lobby until midnight shaking the hands of one and all. Had it been me, I would have been up in the bathtub with my book, happy that the day was over. It is the difference between an introvert and an extrovert. Hubert got his batteries recharged by shaking hands, while my batteries recharged in solitude and reading a book.

The success of our "Bury Goldwater" hootenanny inspired Harry Tuft to come to me and propose we act as impresario to a certain group in Denver. Harry had arranged a loan at a bank but needed a cosigner. The first rule of being a lawyer is not to borrow or loan, but I did cosign the note to the bank. We rented the old Denver Auditorium, obligating ourselves to several thousand more dollars, and tried to sell tickets. Practically nothing. A dribble of sales. No interest in our group, which was not as well-known as we had thought. We were looking at a disaster!

The Monday before the performance, *Time Magazine* had our group on the cover. The Mamas and the Papas and their songs were working their way up the music charts. Talk about luck! The phones rang off the hook, we opened up another sales office, and by the night of concert we knew we had a great success. They were a huge hit.

After the performance, we had a cast party, and it was the first time I ever saw people smoking funny cigarettes and my first experience with marijuana. One of our ticket agents ran off with four thousand dollars, but we managed to pay back our loan, pay for the venue, and still make a lot of money.

After that, we brought in Judy Collins and Ravi Shankar and made money on both. Little did we know the promise of this business, and the vacuum we left by our myopia was soon filled by rock-concert mogul Barry Fey. Oh, well…

Harry Tuft remains a close friend to this day. I met him as I walked home from my accounting job in 1962, and the Folklore Center became a place I would go after work to relax in the mood of the beatnik and folk music movement. Work filling out tax returns all day then chill at the Folklore Center. Perfect balance.

RUNNING FOR THE LEGISLATURE

During the summer and fall of 1966, I was busy campaigning for one of Denver's legislative seats. Lord, I loved that first legislative campaign. The fall of 1966 was before Vietnam split the Democratic Party. All of Denver was the election district, and I got to go to Italian dinners, Black churches, Hispanic dances, and German polka parties at the Denver Turnverein. Dottie would often accompany me, and it became a family project. I won the election easily and arranged my newly minted law practice to accommodate serving in the legislature.

Early in January 1967, I walked into the Colorado House chambers. I was thirty-one years old and was awed. It is hard not to be awed by the House chambers, and I certainly never thought I would go any higher. I had only been in Colorado for five years, I had limited money, and I knew no one of importance in the entire state. I was audacious, but so were the other hundred legislators. How could I best serve my constituents? How would I ever make my mark? My world was very frenetic with my law practice, the legislature, and my family. Dottie, as always, was a great help. Answering the constantly ringing phone, cooking meals, making coffee and cookies for volunteers, and hosting a series of beer parties in our basement. Meanwhile, she was working as a psychiatric social worker with challenged young people, which often weighed on her. Life was like drinking out of a fire hydrant. But I was happy, and both Dottie and I loved our life.

I was involved in an array of issues during those years. I tried to get some land use planning legislation and tried to get a 5 cents deposit on glass bottles and was deeply involved in most of the environmental legislation.

In 1969 a Chicago group, "The First National Conference on Environment and Population," asked me to be their president. I accepted and we organized a large conference in Chicago at which Dennis Hayes announced the first Earth Day. It was not a paid job and it involved at least one weekend a month back in Chicago. In the course of these duties I flew back and forth to Chicago more times than I want to remember. We had a wonderful conference and helped publicize a wide range of environmental issues. Paul Ehrlich asked me to be on the board of Zero Population Growth and then when he stepped down, asked me to be the next president. More trips around the nation but speaking and working on issues I felt deeply about.

It was a yeasty and exciting time in my life. In a shift that was seldom seen in Demography, the population growth rate plummeted. The birth rate headed down starting in 1964 and stayed down. Women had access to contraception and (in many states) abortion and we were successful and even smug. We had been bit players in an incredible social movement.

Dottie meanwhile was actively involved in the Woman's movement and was mentoring a number of young women in politics and in life generally. Both of us actively involved in a variety of issues, raising children and enjoying a busy and productive life.

One example was the issue of dams in the Grand Canyon. In 1963, I had taken a raft trip down the Colorado River just as the gates to the Glen Canyon Dam were closing creating Lake Powell. We put the trip together ourselves and were able to see the wondrous rock formations later depicted in the Sierra Club book "The Place No One Knew." When the Corp. of Engineers proposed in 1969 two additional dams in the Grand Canyon we formed a national group that eventually helped save the Grand Canyon from those dams. I flew back to Washington D.C. to testify before Mo Udall's committee against the dams and got to know even better David Brower who had been the head of the Sierra Club for years. David had offered me a job in 1961 just as I was finishing at Berkeley but I turned him down mainly because I wanted to work in the civil rights area and didn't want to live in California. I could see already how crowded and congested it was becoming. I always had Colorado in the back of my mind, but at the time of graduation I was open to anyplace that wasn't California. Three thousand people a day were moving into California during those years. Traffic, smog, and congestion were defacing that beautiful state.

My eight years in the legislature were some of the happiest in my life. Heather was born, Scott was thriving, and I loved the University of Denver and loved my role in the legislature. My life was incredibly busy but it had a certain balance to it.

GETTING ESTABLISHED IN DENVER

The Young Democrats wasn't the only activity I got involved in after moving to Denver. For instance, I also joined Toastmasters, a civic group dedicated to making people better public speakers. The possibility of a career as a trial lawyer was always a prospect for me. I was covering more than one base.

Every Monday night about fifty of us, mostly men at first, would meet for dinner. Two members would be asked in advance to make an eight- to ten-minute speech, and the rest of us would be randomly chosen without notice and given a subject

ROCK CLIMBING IN BOULDER

to speak on for two minutes. Questions ranged widely, ranging from "How will the Broncos do next season?" to "What should the US policy be toward Cuba?" Great way to develop extemporaneous speaking skills, but very intimidating. I learned a great deal about speaking from Toastmasters, but it was finally crowded out by Young Democrats and by my growing confidence in my own speaking ability. Toastmasters worked!

I also started a Conservation section of the Colorado Mountain Club. Dottie and I spent a lot of weekends with the Colorado Mountain Club, but as we began to feel more confident in the mountains, the two of us climbed increasingly without the club.

I have always had a sense of finiteness. From college on, I have thought that suburbs were ugly, inefficient, and a false hope. That growth of population and the economy could not go on forever. My parents had been big supporters of Planned Parenthood, so part of it was in my upbringing. The sign "Watch Us Grow!," which was on billboards outside many towns in America, always made me think and speculate. Is that really what the citizens of that town wanted? Watching Madison or San Francisco or Denver grow, it was always alarming to me, and I certainly felt it to be an aesthetic insult. Was this development necessary? Was it well planned and designed? It always seemed to me we gave away our open space too easily. Local government is always too easily seduced by development.

But by far the larger issue for me was how to stabilize the population, both worldwide and in the United States, and to find a way to develop a sustainable economy.

I also realized early on that "finiteness" was important in planning your career and life. We do not live forever, and the knowledge that someday we die is key to knowing how to live. We only get one chance and it is important to think about how we spend our limited time.

THE ABORTION DEBATE

Once I was immersed in politics, democracy clearly worked for me. And looking back on my career, I see I had one trait that, more than any other, made me successful in that arena. It sounds self-serving—even a brag—so I can understand the reader's skepticism, but I believe I succeeded because I fought for what I believed in. And while I acknowledge that history is filled with people in life and politics who go down in flames while fighting for an issue about which they're passionate, it is a lesson that is important for the current generation to learn, quixotic as it may sound. I believe that, more than any skill or trait, fighting for what I believed in was what propelled me in my political career. In addition, my timing was auspicious: when I was first elected to the Colorado legislature, I looked for a way to make the world a better place. Dottie and I had lived in South America for six months after we got married in May of 1963, in often-primitive conditions, traveled by bus to many remote areas, and learned in our travels that generally in South America one-quarter of the hospital beds were taken up by women who had had botched abortions. We had met and talked with the Marino fathers of the Catholic Church who were handing out birth control to their parishioners in Peru because, despite the church's ban on artificial birth control, "It was clearly less sinful than abortion," which they admitted was an epidemic. Dottie, a nascent feminist even then, was particularly and personally outraged. "How can the law force unwilling women to have unwanted children?" Most of these victims already had large families and were desperate to limit the number of children they had, but who had no alternative other than illegal abortion, usually performed by someone without medical training. Birth control was generally illegal both in Peru and all of South America because of the Catholic Church. We saw the male-dominated oligarchy, where the same small group of families sent one son to the family business, one to politics, and one to the church, monopolize most of the wealth and political power and then produce policies that killed or ruined thousands of women who felt they could not adequately care for an additional child. We saw clearly in South America, and still believe today, that the law can't say whether a woman will have an abortion, it can only say where. Desperate women, following their own conscience, were going to prevent unwanted pregnancies one way or another. South America was Exhibit A for this viewpoint.

The art of passing successful legislation is the practice of marshaling—and in some cases manufacturing—the necessary support for attainable goals. In a representative government, responding as it must to the wishes of the constituents, legislation is by necessity closely tied up with public opinion. Al Smith, one of the world's most practical politicians, stated it thus: "A politician can't be so far ahead of the band he can't hear the music." It can, by definition, be no other way. No politician who is too far out front of public opinion will survive politically.

The passage in 1967 of Colorado's abortion reform law, the first in the nation and seven years prior to *Roe v. Wade*, is an excellent case study in the advantages and limitations of the legislative process. Colorado's old law on abortion was put on the books while Colorado was still under a territorial legislature and was atypical from the start. Colorado was one of the five states whose law went beyond permitting abortions only to save the life of the mother. Its law included as grounds for abortion not only the need to save the mother's life but also the need to save her from "substantial risk of bodily harm." From all the statistics available, however, Colorado's number of abortions, even with the broader parameters, was similar to the national average. In the ten years preceding the passage of the new law, one of Denver's major hospitals had performed only forty-nine abortions—an average of approximately five per year. This was a ratio of 1 to 418 births, which compared with the average ratio in all US hospitals as reported by nationally available statistics. The grounds given even for these few abortions were such that it was obvious that doctors were stretching the old law.

Now, fifty years later, I cannot remember who called the first meeting on changing the law to which I was invited; I know it wasn't me. Ruth Steel, a wonderful and dedicated woman who had been instrumental in passing a birth control access law for women on welfare, was present, as were some professors from the Colorado Health Sciences Center and some liberal clergy. Someone had heard Dottie and me describing our experience in South America with its cruel burden of anti-abortion laws, and the purpose of this meeting was to see if someone would introduce a liberalized abortion law. No one in the room believed it had any chance of passing that year, but it was thought that the subject should be broached so it could be reviewed in future legislatures. I was understandably cautious about the idea, although I had never thought of politics as more than a brief avocation. It was assumed that what was thought of as a largely symbolic act would be a heavy burden to the legislative sponsors in any upcoming elections. I was told honestly and candidly that I was to be a "sacrificial Lamm." I was a freshman legislator and hardly knew where my seat was in the legislative chambers.

But we felt that it at least had to be introduced and the conversation started. Two years before, Colorado had succeeded in passing, on a second attempt, a law that provided birth control information to indigent women. On the first attempt at the birth control legislation, the bill never left committee, but on its second introduction, it passed by a fairly substantial margin. The public's acceptance of that law had gone some distance in paving the way for abortion reform in the minds of the legislators. The birth control law had been passed, signed by the governor, put into operation, and forgotten. Most legislators were aware that in that case, the storms of adverse reaction passed without raining retribution. But we didn't kid ourselves. Abortion, we knew, would be a much more volatile issue.

The prevailing opinion at the meeting was one of realism, if not pessimism, because it was our feeling that the attempt to change the law at the time might well hurt more than help the eventual passage of a liberalizing law. There is nothing that so scares legislators collectively than to see a measure soundly defeated in the legislative process, and its proponent defeated at the polls. Timing is extremely important in the passing of successful legislation, and an ill-advised, premature attempt often has the effect of substantially delaying a law's eventual passage.

A young law student, Susan Graham (whom I later appointed a Denver District Court judge as Susan Barnes), had done a class project in law school on liberalized abortion, and we decided on her general form of the legislation. We wanted to argue that we were only slightly expanding the categories under which an abortion could be obtained, while at the same time tightening the circumstances under which it would be performed. We decided to expand the grounds of legal abortion to include physical health, mental health, rape, incest, and fetal deformity. Two doctors had to certify that one of those conditions was present.

I agreed to approach a few legislators for their reactions, and the more legislators I approached, the more a cautious optimism began to grow. Ruth Steel, always dressed as if going to church and with a kindly and ladylike personality covering an iron determination, then joined me in approaching legislators. Ruth actually knew the legislators better than I did because of her good work on the birth control legislation. She and I also requested state senator John Birmingham, the brilliant and effective sponsor of the birth control legislation, to help us take the temperature of the legislature.

Ruth and I started by approaching the Protestant and Jewish members of the legislature we thought would be most receptive. We all did it with apprehension because *abortion* was not even a word to use in polite company. It was not a word ever heard on the news and seldom read in the paper. It was truly a taboo subject, so we were amazed when we compared notes a day later to find that all six people we approached that day felt some variation of "the time had come" to face this subject. Most of them said they would cosponsor the legislation, something we had not even asked at this stage. Fortified and encouraged by this response, we started approaching all the legislators and asking for a commitment.

Certain issues lend themselves to partisan appeal; others are by nature nonpartisan. Abortion law reform is by its nature nonpartisan, and our ad hoc committee worked hard to keep it that way. Representative Carl Gustafson, a Republican from Denver, manifested a great interest in the legislation and, along with me, agreed to be the prime cosponsor in the House.

Always brave, Senator John Birmingham signed on to be the chief sponsor in the Senate. The die was cast.

Together we ascertained that on a bill bound to be this controversial it would be necessary to get twenty cosponsors out of the one hundred Colorado legislators to assure us that in the likely event of defeat we would at least set a base of support for the future. Together with these other two intrepid legislators, we put on a full-court press. To our great surprise—and absolute amazement—virtually every legislator we approached not only agreed to put his/her name on the bill but expressed great enthusiasm. When we were finished quietly contacting the various legislators, we had a total of sixty-three cosponsors, more than half in the House of Representatives and slightly less than half of the Senate.

After the initial stages of contacting the legislators, and when it was apparent that there was a much greater chance for successful passage of this legislation than we had originally anticipated, Representative Gustafson and I called our ad hoc committee to discuss the different possibilities of marshaling public opinion behind this law. We were well aware that the subject of legalized abortion, long taboo, would meet with extremely stiff opposition, and we realized how important it was to have the various community opinion molders on the side of change. We invited members of the clergy whom we knew were sympathetic to the law, along with a significant number of doctors to serve both as our advisors and counselors. We immediately formed a committee of clergy and charged it with the express duty of contacting fellow clergy members of all faiths and getting them to specifically endorse the new bill. We also set up the machinery of appearing before the Colorado Council of Churches in an attempt to get an endorsement from that body. At the same time, we charged the doctors with the duty of building a medical committee of doctors whose names we could publicly use as endorsing the new legislation.

We then decided to approach the news media and seek their endorsement, or at least their understanding. At the time, the news media were the single most important factor in shaping community opinion with regard to legislation. It was deemed imperative by us to at least negate opposition on the part of the press, and if possible to seek specific endorsement of the proposed legislation from them. For this purpose, a panel was formed consisting of Representative Gustafson and myself representing the two political parties, and a doctor and minister or rabbi representing their respective viewpoints. This ad hoc group called upon all the major news media in the Denver area and explained our bill to them. Any medical questions were answered by the doctor, any moral issues were taken on by the clergy, any legislative question by the two legislators. The effort proved immensely successful and won us enthusiastic support during the legislative battle in the form of three editorials by the *Denver Post*.

With the cosponsors in place, it remained only to ensure sympathetic committee assignments in the legislature. The leadership of both the House and the Senate can well defeat legislation by assigning it to a committee where it knows it will be buried. We thus approached he leadership of both the House and the Senate and requested the bill's assignment to the Health and Welfare Committees, which we had previously ascertained would give us at least a fair hearing. With the assurances from the leadership of the necessary committee assignment, our bill was introduced.

Pandemonium. Individual letters from all over Colorado, mostly in opposition, hit the desks of the legislators, and many of them were contacted individually by phone. The committee chair in the House, where the bill was introduced, waited for the initial storm to pass before calling hearing on the legislation. We determined to use as proponents of the legislation the most conservative and responsible people we had at our disposal. I sadly had to turn down my own pastor, who had married Dottie and me, because he was a Unitarian and thus predictably liberal. We picked ministers, doctors, and lawyers who had not previously been involved in controversial legislation of any kind and had the best of credentials. We choreographed the hearings as if they were a stage play, with the right themes at the right time, often to rebut a known opponent. At the House committee hearing, twenty-three testified in favor of the legislation and nineteen against. The bill was voted out of committee.

Yes, we said over and over again, a fetus is a potential human being. But in no area of public policy did we equate the potential with the actual. A student in K–12 education has the "potential" to graduate but isn't called a "graduate" until he/she has gone through all the steps. An acorn is not an oak tree; burning a blueprint of a house is different from burning an actual house. And so it went, and so it still goes today.

At this point, we felt it necessary to help offset all the adverse mail coming to the legislators on the subject. To do this, we asked each of the twenty-three people who testified in favor of the legislation to distill their testimony into writing, and at the start of each legislative day we laid one or two copies of this testimony on the desks of all one hundred legislators. Thus, each day upon his/her desk, each legislator had some supporting testimony from a responsible source to help offset their negative mail. In addition, we reproduced some of the better articles on the subject and put these on the legislators' desks as well. We then set up a network so we could get doctors and clergy in each legislator's district to call with their support. It was our opinion that one letter from a doctor or clergy member was worth twenty adverse letters. The campaign proved to be very successful. The medical profession really found its voice, and a long list of doctors subscribed to our list of proponents, which we distributed widely.

It was extremely helpful to proponents of this legislation that all of those supporting the bill agreed upon the particular provisions at the outset, and none caused the added controversy of attempting to make it even more liberal. All were agreed that the bill as introduced would be a substantial and advantageous reform of the existing abortion laws, and that we would only succeed if all proponents backed the same specific piece of legislation; the dichotomy existing between those favoring change in a state such as California seemed to hinder the passage of any reform legislation at all. We were very hardheaded on what we could accomplish.

The polls showed at the time what our practical experience taught us—that the public was at the time a long way from accepting an absence of all restrictions whatsoever upon a doctor's authority to approve an abortion. Society felt that they still had a role in dictating circumstances under which an abortion was to be performed. It was easy in Colorado to argue that the moral issues raised by the opponents of this legislation had long been resolved in the United States; in other words, that under some circumstances any woman may obtain an abortion to protect her life. To those arguments that the new law was "taking a life" and thus was unconstitutional, we had the easy retort that no one had ever challenged the constitutionality of any of the other state's abortion laws, including Colorado's, and all we were doing was slightly expanding the categories under which an abortion could be obtained while at the same time tightening the circumstances under which it could be performed. When the question is put as merely a weighing of two rights—between the health and welfare of the mother and the potential human personality of the fetus—the public seemed conformable and satisfied. We stuck close to what our best judgment told us could be accomplished.

We next anticipated what would be the principal amendments offered by the opposition to the bill and chose individual legislators to handle the opposition to the weakening amendments. All major attempts at amending the bill on the floor of the House were eventually defeated, and the bill was voted out of the House, going to the Senate in substantially the same form as introduced and passed by the committee. The legislative history of the bill in the Senate was substantially the same as in the House. The bill passed, and after the House concurred in a minor amendment, the bill was sent to the governor for his signature. We had done it!

I thought my role was over, but the wise representative Rich Gebhardt from Boulder said no, and we spent a solid week getting important people to write the governor in support.

He taught me to never, never, never take anything for granted in the legislative process. Governor John A. Love signed the legislation, and Colorado became the first state in the nation to liberalize its abortion legislation. A majority of Republicans in both chambers and a Republican governor passed a law that unfortunately kicked off an ideological war within the Republican Party that still echoes today.

It was a heady trip for a thirty-two-year-old. My picture was in *Time Magazine* as well as significant other national press. I was named Outstanding Freshman Legislator and got invited to testify in Texas, New York, Kansas, and some other states on behalf of their own attempts to change their laws. I was also adopted by a number of abortion rights groups and got to make speeches and testify to legislatures around the country as well as speak at dinners and meetings of feminists, public health people, and organizations in favor of liberalizing their abortion laws. In the space of six or seven years, abortion had gone from being mostly illegal everywhere to mostly legal in a number of states. I had made a significant number of both enemies and friends, but more than anything I had learned how to succeed in the legislative process. From this point on, nothing to me could match the excitement and rewards of public policy. I was hooked.

Ironically, this issue has not only not gone away, it has exploded into a continuing hot button issue that shows no sign of abating. It is a bigger issue politically today than it was in 1967 and seemingly beyond compromise. It still drives political debate and endless secular argument. It seems the obvious compromise is to allow us all to follow our own conscience on such a sensitive matter, but the anti-abortion movement continues to seek to impose its view on everyone.

SECOND LEGISLATIVE CAMPAIGN

My legislative home in Denver was District 8, which, in 1968, had a Republican incumbent, Lila Gilbert. I had to first win the Democratic nomination, and that required me to personally call on all the district captains and win their support. That proved easier than I feared because of Marjorie Major, who worked tirelessly for my campaign and without whom I never would have won the district. She took a massive amount of time to brief me, sharing with me the dynamic of the district. Marjorie was about forty, a Catholic mother of five kids, and married to a Public Service (the state's utilities provider) employee. She was a lovely lady, and I will never be able to thank her enough. With her guidance and help, I avoided a primary and won the seat in November of 1968, despite the ten thousand pictures of bottled fetuses that Lila Gilbert, my Republican opponent, distributed throughout the district. That January I was elected assistant minority leader to serve behind Tom Farley of Pueblo, who was elected minority leader.

One day in early 1969, the dean of the University of Denver (DU) School of Law came to see me with the offer of a faculty position. Dean Bob Yegge offered me a full faculty position, and my main duties would be to run the Student Practice Program where students would, while still in law school, take pro bono cases and build their skills. Being in the legislature was not a problem because that added to the real world he was trying to bring to the law school. He said he wanted to show the students they could impact the legal system and the world, as I had just done via the abortion legislation. This was a difficult time in higher education. The Vietnam War had infected a whole generation with cynicism and nihilism, and America was just barely holding on to its draft-age young people. I hired as my deputy Howard Gelt, who himself had only recently graduated from University of Denver law. Howard worked magic with the students and soon became a trusted political advisor. I stand on the shoulders of some wonderful people.

THE DARK SIDE OF MY WIFE, DOTTIE LAMM

I still often wonder how I could have been so lucky to have met my wife, Dottie. A long life has some thirty thousand to forty thousand days and nights, most of them unremarkable. Productive days, fun days, but hard to bring back individually. I shall, however, never forget the night I met Dottie. It is, of course, seared into my memory. However, in furtherance of an honest memoir, there is something I should disclose.

IN THE GOVERNOR'S MANSION, 1976

Dottie and I courted by skiing that winter and climbing Colorado's high mountains the summer of 1962. We would often climb two 14,000-foot mountains on a weekend. How can you not fall in love with a beautiful woman who held you safely at the end of a one-hundred-foot rope?

I proposed that the two of us join a mountain-climbing expedition in South America, but she didn't want to go unless we were married. "Married!" That severely offended my sense of hippiness. It was absolute bourgeoisie bullshit. "Only a damn piece of paper," I stormed, "marriage is passé," and so on. I was boringly conventional in my unconventionality, embarrassingly trite in my anti-authoritarianism. What do you expect from a guy from Berkeley?

But I did love her deeply, so I gave in. So much for good deeds, though! No sooner had I given in to this deeply offensive, archaic practice than she hit me with another blow: she wanted her parents at the wedding! What middle-class bullshit! I had already given up and compromised part of my revolutionary soul by agreeing to ask the state for permission to live with the woman I loved, and now this? I had to draw the line somewhere before I found myself living in the suburbs and belonging to a country club. "Absolutely not, Dottie, I have a judge who will marry us in chambers, and there is no way I am publicly assenting to this intrusive state overreaching practice. No, NO, NO WAY.

We were married in the Unitarian church on May 11, 1963, with our parents and two couples we climbed with in attendance. Immediately afterward, we set off to Peru for our honeymoon and a climbing expedition.

It was in Lima, Peru, shortly after we joined our expedition and about a month after we were married when Dottie showed her dark side. It casts such a bad reflection on her that I still hesitate to air publicly our dirty family laundry, and I guarantee you will never feel the same about Dottie Lamm. I admit that I have always been a of a tightwad, but this way beyond the bounds! I still, more than fifty years later, get upset, and part of me can never forget because … because … because one afternoon as I was busy loading equipment onto our expedition truck she went out and bought—a six-dollar can of hairspray. Six dollars! Hairspray! "Vanity, thy name is women." We had budgeted two dollars a day for bumming around South America after our climbing trip, and here she went out and for frivolous, vain, and totally unnecessary reasons had essentially cut our trip short by three days. I ranted, I raved. I tried to get her to return it. I told her I would never sleep with her if she had on hairspray, and she only smiled that damn sardonic smile of hers, which threw me into further fits of rage.

She never did return the hairspray, and we did have children, so in a sense I backed down. I know you must also be shocked and amazed at her unnecessary extravagance, but she has turned out to be a pretty good wife. Due mainly, I would suggest, to my great qualities of being an understanding and sensitive husband.

LEGISLATIVE YEARS

I loved being in the legislature and loved being assistant minority leader (the "whip"), and it was a hectic but fruitful time in my life. I got invited to testify before the New York legislature on liberalizing abortion laws. The N.Y. legislative chambers were filled with history, and the big, cavernous hearing room was packed with both proponents and opponents of abortion. I was also invited to Austin, Texas, to testify before the Texas legislature, and this is where I first met Sarah Weddington, who a few years later took *Roe vs. Wade* to the US Supreme Court and won an astounding victory for reproductive freedom. Dottie and I have kept in contact with Sarah for these many years, and she occasionally stays with us when in Denver. I was also invited to a number of other out-of-state meetings and events to tell the Colorado story.

I was involved in two large legal battles while in the legislature and loved the fact that I was fighting for good things, both in the legislature and the courts. The first battle, in 1971, was when the federal government announced as part of Project Plowshare a plan to explode nuclear devices in western Colorado to blast more oil and gas out of our shale. Project Plowshare's goal was to make much larger civilian use of our nuclear arsenal and atomic research. Plowshare had raised the idea of making new harbors along the West Coast, building canals by exploding small nuclear devices, and so forth. My brother Tom and I were approached by a group of environmentalists to try and stop the event. They were appalled at the possibility of ten to twenty nuclear explosions going off in various parts of Colorado. The case, of course, would be pro bono, and ultimately we had to eat a large part of the costs. I had met an environmental attorney from Long Island named Victor Yannacone, and we invited him to join us. Again, pro bono. We filed our case in the Federal District Court trying to get an injunction against even the first explosion, which was to be held seventy-six miles north of Grand Junction, Colorado. We were immediately answered by a major Houston law firm, and the judge set a date in the near future. We found an expert at the University of Pittsburgh who claimed a number of negative environmental consequences could/would flow from this program, and in the hearing we put on our expert who had an impressive academic record but who didn't impress Judge Alfred Aaraj at all. Our injunction was denied, and the explosion went ahead, followed by a second explosion, also in northwest Colorado.

The lawsuit did draw attention, and the press covered the trial well, awakening a number of people to the fact that literally thousands of nuclear explosions were proposed to go off underground in Colorado. Public opposition grew rapidly as we contemplated an appeal. Before the appeal needed to be filed we were told by an insider that the gas created by the explosion was (surprise) radioactive and not suitable for domestic use. Both the Plowshare Oil and Gas programs became infeasible, and virtually all the other Plowshare programs were dropped as impractical or infeasible.

Our ragged team had lost the battle but won the war! I continue to believe our theory of the case, which was that the tritium released had a significant chance of ending up in the Colorado River. Tritium is a heavy hydrogen, and contamination could occur even in stagnant groundwater and ultimately contaminate both Colorado's river system and groundwater. It is not an event that many people recall, but it is important to remember that the proposal at one time talked about hundreds of nuclear devices being exploded under Colorado.

The second case was more successful, if more improbable. In south-central Colorado, a land developer was commencing development of a subdivision on some land that the scientists had shown held invaluable and irreplaceable fossils. Few people know how special they were, but a diverse group of Coloradoans who recognized the values of these fossils came to my brother Tom and me and asked for help. The bulldozers were already on the land, only a couple of days from starting to scrape away these irreplaceable fossils. I called the developer who refused even to take my phone call. Brother Tom immediately called Victor Yannacone who dropped everything and was on the next plane. We got a bill introduced in Congress that would have purchased the land. This, of course, was key to our victory, for the judge knew that the developer had a buyer. We went far into the night preparing pleadings, and we filed at the federal courthouse the moment it was open. We sent a process server down south to serve the developer and asked for an immediate hearing. Judge William Doyle gave us a temporary restraining order and set a date for a hearing. The developer cried bloody murder. "What gave us any rights to his land?" — a point that was hard to refute. Victor Yannacone argued passionately to the judge, saying that if a copy of the US Constitution were buried in a place about to be bulldozed, the court would find a way to stop the bulldozers. We argued that this was a valid analogy: these were priceless fossils unique to the world, and they were about to be destroyed, forever.

And it would indeed have been a significant loss to the natural world. The Florissant Formation, the area targeted by the development, is composed of alternating units of shale, mudstone, conglomerate, and volcanic deposits. In the late Eocene to early Oligocene eras, approximately 34 million years ago, this area was a lake. There are six described units within the Florissant Formation, and each of the shale units represents different environments composed of very thin shales that are abundant in fossils. The separation of the shale units by non-lake deposits could mean that there were two generations of lake deposits available for study. It was truly a unique and irreplaceable geography.

The judge gave us the preliminary injunction, and then just sat on the pleadings. He did nothing. The owner/developer was outraged, as he had a whole crew in place and ready to go. The judge then set a hearing for the day after the legislation would pass Congress. The bill passed, the hearing was held, and the developer seemed to understand the direction in which the judge was going. Just wait. Stall. Wait for Congress to act. The developer clearly owned the land, but Judge Doyle knew the power of delay, and it worked!

In the end, Congress passed the legislation, the developer got paid, and the Florissant National Monument was created. Right outside park headquarters is a plaque with the names of the two Lamm brothers and Victor Yannacone and the thanks of the park sponsors. Lovely, given that many issues I had worked for years on went nowhere. In Florissant, I spent two heart-stopping weeks and got my name on a plaque. I loved the fact that I was changing public policy both in the legislature and in the courts. I felt a growing sense of accomplishment and pride in the life I had chosen and worked hard for.

AN OLYMPIAN BATTLE

Because of my accounting background I was appointed to the Audit Committee of the Legislature, and two years later, in 1969, I was appointed chair of the Audit Committee. The Audit Committee and the Joint Budget Committee were the only legislative committees that a minority party member could chair. In my eight years in the legislature, I never once served in the majority.

It was in the capacity of my role on the Audit Committee that I started looking at the costs of a potential 1976 winter Olympics to be held in Denver, which became a top priority after Denver won the bid to be the host city. The more I looked, the more concerned I became. My friend, Representative Bob Jackson of Pueblo, was also on the Audit Committee and shared my concern. It soon became apparent that the Denver Organizing Committee hadn't begun to grasp all that was involved in hosting the Winter Olympics, and was both seriously overestimating the revenue and dramatically underestimating the costs. At some point I took these figures to Michael Howard, scion of the Howard in Scripps Howard Publishing and others at the *Rocky Mountain News* and to Don Seawell, the publisher of the *Denver Post*. Don Seawell was totally negative on the subject and seemed to imply that I wasn't showing adequate civic commitment to Colorado. I got the impression he was struggling even to be civil to me. The *Rocky Mountain News*'s Michael Howard was a true newspaper man who assigned a top reporter to the issue. The *News* ran a stunning series of articles that essentially confirmed what we had been saying and more.

I was very busy with DU, my family, and the legislature, when who should appear but Sam Brown, one of the five key organizers of the entire antiwar movement in the mid-1960s.

Sam moved right in and volunteered to help. How exactly we found our other key organizers, Tom Nussbaum, Meg Lundstrom, and John Parr, is lost from my memory (in fact, they found us), but Sam Brown had an acquaintance who he said had deep pockets and was interested in what we were doing. One short meeting with this deep pocket and we had enough money to open an office, pay some modest salaries, start other fund-raising, and print some literature.

As soon as the press published our organizational phone number, the phone started ringing off the hook, and volunteers were coming into the office in such numbers that it interfered with getting our staff work done. A young Denverite, Dwight Filley, a college student taking some time off of school, joined our team as a volunteer. Again, I stood on the shoulders of others: Tom Nussbaum, Meg Lundstrom, John Parr, and Sam Brown in particular. They were pure magic but also incredibly smart and hardworking.

The whole campaign unfolded with the *Rocky Mountain News* acting as an honest journalistic organization and the *Denver Post* as an unquestioning cheerleader for the Olympics. Luge runs in Evergreen where there was seldom snow, a ski jump miles from any other venues, significant transportation challenges, costs constantly going up. We somehow found the money to send a delegation to Sapporo, Japan, where the 1972 Olympics were being held, and by clever and aggressive actions they got to present our petitions against holding the Olympics in Denver to the International Olympics Committee. I debated Carl De Temple of the Denver Chamber of Commerce to a wide audience on Rocky Mountain PBS. Throughout it all, Brown, Nussbaum, Parr, Lundstrom, and Filley were organizing volunteers and doing the hard work of political organizing. They were incredible, and we caught all the breaks. We collected the necessary signatures, and when voters cast their ballots in November 1972, they turned down state funding for the Olympics 60 percent to 40 percent; they also elected Pat Schroeder to the House of Representatives, the first woman from Colorado to serve in that role. At a victory party the night of the vote, one of our volunteers, community activist John Zappien, held me up to the ceiling and said, "Ladies and gentlemen, the next governor of Colorado!" I looked around at all the dedicated people and realized he might be right. Here we had a mailing list of dedicated people, a fund-raising list, and lots of people who wanted to help. It was doable.

Sam Brown had a similar idea and started putting together a campaign for state treasurer. Sam had done all these marvelous things, but had not yet established a political home. I had been in Colorado fewer than twelve years, Sam fewer than that. The establishment repeated the mistake of the Olympics: they dismissed us as unimportant, but we were plowing new ground. Large megaprojects such as the Olympics (sports stadiums, etc.) had generally passed easily in Colorado and other states. I was ahead of my time, but I sensed that voters were at this point becoming more and more skeptical about large megaprojects. In addition, the "Watch Us Grow" Chamber of Commerce message was increasingly met with opposition.

2. ON THE ROAD TO GOVERNORSHIP

INTERREGNUM

I graduated from the University of Wisconsin in June of 1957 with a degree in accounting and, more importantly, an appreciation of how ignorant I was. What a gift! I had begun to understand what a wonderful and complex world it was and what fascinating creatures inhabited it. I knew enough to know that I didn't know very much, and that inspired me to develop a program of continuing education, mostly by reading good books.

I had a "Road from Damascus" moment that had a profound impact on my life. I hashed every weekday evening and Sunday noon at the Tri Delta House. On campus in the middle of my sophomore year, I ran into a young lady from Tri Delta and asked her to coffee. "Can't," she replied. "I have a class. Come with me to my class."

I did, and that class changed my life. We took seats toward the front, and soon this little white-haired old lady, Professor Helen White, stood up and started to talk about someone named Shakespeare. "Life changing," because I realized while I was stuck in the business school (marketing, urban land economics), many of my fellow students were taking history, literature, and, yes—Shakespeare. I left that class and immediately figured out how to expand my horizons. I still stayed in accounting but was soon taking creative writing, history, and literature. A deeper, more creative and aware student was born. I went into law school as a college senior but continued to read widely and even audit some classes in liberal arts. I am still a student to this day.

"Sliding doors" became a metaphor for a few key events in my life. Call it fate, serendipity, karma, luck—events happen in all lives that in retrospect had major impact on their course. The fact that I am not a religious man makes the capriciousness of the sliding door so perfect. What if…

As I discussed in Chapter 1, who I married almost certainly hung on a party invitation; the likelihood of meeting Dottie was otherwise slim. Denver was a pretty big town with lots of young people. It would have been unlikely that I would have ever met her after that night.

But the fact that I became governor hung on another sliding door. On an oppressively hot night back in the summer of 1973, Richard Young, the state Democratic chair, brought together Mark Hogan, Tom Farley, and me—at the time, all candidates for Colorado governor—in his office in Denver's Brooks Tower. Dick announced that his three strongest candidates were all running for governor, and the party had no strong candidate running for the US senate. He said he would wait there, all night if necessary, until one of us dropped out of the governor's race and ran for the Senate instead.

Each of us made our case for why we wanted to run for governor and why we didn't want to run for senator. We spent four hours talking and debating, but by midnight we all were exhausted and decided to go home, with no one moved from their position.

On the way home, I reviewed the evening. Here I was essentially being offered the US Senate nomination (Dick Young would strongly back whichever one of us would switch to the Senate race) instead of being faced with a tough primary for the governor's nomination. I was hot, exhausted, and increasingly uncertain. Why not take the path of least resistance? I needed to talk it out with Dottie.

SEEING THE WORLD

Dottie and I were married in May of 1963 and then spent six months in South America. We climbed some very big mountains, which required us to carry ropes and mountaineering gear. We had an average of two dollars a day to live on, but we had our sleeping bags and would often go the best hotel in town late at night and sleep in the lawn shrubbery, which also gave us a safe place to sleep. In the morning, we would go into the hotel to see if we could sneak in a shower. Being Anglos, we seldom got challenged as we wandered around the hotel looking for bathing facilities.

We went from Peru by train to Argentina, then to Iguazu Falls on the border of Argentina and Brazil. Then it was on to Manaus on the Amazon River, and by boat for a week to Belen on the mouth of the Amazon. On to Venezuela and then Bolivia and Colombia, where we visited Bogotá and Cartagena, an old pirate town dating from 1533 complete with narrow streets and lots of charm.

When we got back from our honeymoon and climbing trip to South America, we started to look for a house. We found a wonderful old house (originally a farmhouse) at 531 Emerson, now the heart of Capitol Hill in Denver. We bought it for $11,900 and steamed off the ancient wallpaper, built bookcases, and refurbished the kitchen. We made it into a lovely and homey home, and it was there where I ran and won my first election. We loved that house and thought it would last us at least through two children. But then the legislature happened, and the abortion bill happened, and then a constitutional amendment uprooted our lives.

COLD DUCK

This choice led to my second big sliding door experience, which involved two bottles of wine that were labeled "cold duck." It was the summer of 1973, I was thirty-eight years old, and I was going into my eighth year in the Colorado legislature. To help us decide what my next step should be, I brought home two bottles of cold duck.

I was clearly the most controversial person in the legislature. Many people were urging me to run for governor or the US Senate, and many people thought because of my role in defeating the Olympics that I was a traitor to Colorado and disloyal to the Colorado spirit. Not many subtle colors in my political portrait; it was mostly primary colors.

The trouble with running for governor was that I had a young family. Son Scott was six and daughter Heather was three. In addition, I had little money, and I had offended most of the moneyed interests in Colorado. Oh, yes—the governor's race was further complicated in that I really did like and respect the other democratic contenders, Mark Hogan and Tom Farley.

The sliding door moment occurred when Dottie gave our kids over to the sitter, sat on our living room floor, opened up a bottle of cold duck, and proceeded to discuss what we knew, even then, would be a fateful decision. To run or not to run? US Senate or governor?

Over the first glass of wine, we reviewed our political position. I had offended most of the standard rules of politics. I was, of course, very controversial: witness the Olympics and the nation's first liberalized abortion bill. My legislative seat in south Denver was heavily Catholic, and I had a heavily fought primary and general race every two years. And in 1970 I had started asking questions about Colorado's already successful bid for the 1976 Olympics, and wound up leading a growing, and ultimately successful, movement to prevent any state funding of the Olympics.

On this summer night in July of 1973, it was a real political conundrum: I had many friends and many enemies. What to do? We opened up another bottle of cold duck. Dottie was clearly drinking more than her share.

Second bottle opened, we discussed how I had only lived in Colorado for twelve years, and, in addition to the legislature, I hardly knew the state business leadership, had a struggling legal practice, held a faculty position at DU, and had very little money. I wasn't 100 percent sure that I even had Dottie's vote. What I was known for was controversy, which is hardly the stuff that political careers are made of. But the cold duck made this look more and more manageable, and I did have lots of passionate friends. But which race? Here I was being offered an unobstructed shot at the US Senate that would have

been the dream of millions of aspiring politicians. If I chose to run for governor I could very well lose the primary! But if I won, would that be a life-choice victory? Did I really want to move, even part time, to Washington, D.C.?

PRESS CONFERENCE AT THE STATE CAPITOL

Halfway through the second bottle of cold duck, we decided it would be the governor's race. We had both seen the life of a US Senator, gone from early morning to late at night and little time for family. We had also seen former Colorado governor John Love and his wife, Ann, lead what looked like wonderful family lives in the mansion, with Ann playing an active and vital role in the community. True, it was also filled with long and hectic days, but, if elected governor, I would have much more control over my schedule. The race was still very much a long shot in this Republican state.

We finished the second bottle. The sliding door was closing when I put out my hand and Dottie slapped it: we would roll the political dice for the governorship.

I went into that "family meeting" leaning toward switching to the Senate race. But as we talked and drank, my original doubts came rushing back. Dottie was wonderfully neutral and mainly asked what was best for the kids. We talked of the life of a US senator, and not only was the schedule grueling, Dottie loved living in Colorado and had a women's group and book club and many friends. But she also welcomed new adventures and recognized that if I won either race, the kids would have to enter a new house, new neighborhood, new school, and so on. She did not try and sway me one way or another. The cold duck made a difference. It made me realize that I had taken almost twenty-two years to get to Colorado and that I just didn't want to leave. I called up Dick Young and said I was sticking to the governor's race.

Mark Hogan and Tom Farley had made similar decisions and we were headed for a primary.

TRIP AROUND THE WORLD

Life was coming at us very fast now. We were pregnant and we wanted one more trip before children arrived. I was now working for the Colorado Anti-Discrimination Commission and wanted to run for re-election to the legislature in 1968. We found a district in the bottom half of Denver running from approximately Porter's Hospital to the South Platte and started looking for houses. It was a heavily Catholic area but I didn't have many choices. We would find a home in this district and take our chances. But we could find nothing in the way of houses that appealed to us.

We also decided to go around the world. We learned that if we bought tickets to New Delhi, India, that we could continue around the world with lots of stops along the way. Dottie checked with her doctor who took a dim view of such an unstructured trip but ultimately gave his blessing. The legislature was adjourned from May until the following January and the re-election bid was a year off. We both knew with Dottie pregnant it was our window to get in another trip before our first child arrived. Tickets purchased, notice given to my job, and off we went.

We went to Japan where we stayed first in the historic Imperial Hotel in Tokyo (which was designed by Frank Lloyd Wright), then on to rural Japan where I climbed Mt. Fuji (in street shoes) under a full moon and arrived to watch the sun come up. We next travelled all around Japan including a trip to Hokkaido, the northernmost island of Japan. What a pleasant way to travel! We would arrive at a charming Japanese inn and be given a room with sleeping mats instead of beds. Off to the hot bath which was often communal in those days. (One time we got in and immediately five Japanese got out.) Then into a kimono and served a delicious dinner with hot Saki right in our room). Almost no English in Hokkaido and some of the other towns we visited and we learned to point at what we wanted. We also learned (somewhat) what it means to be discriminated against.

Every part of this trip was special, and we are blessed with exotic memories from that trip. In Sri Lanka we got to the capital city of Colombo to learn that in the town of Kandi the very next day they were having the "Festival of the Tooth" where supposedly one of Buddha's teeth, accompanied by 100 elephants and hundreds of men with whips and burning torches marched down out of the hills under a full moon, in this "Festival of the Tooth." Too tempting to pass up.

But we could get no hotel reservations in Kandy so we took a chance (with Dottie being pregnant) that we would find something. We took the night train to Kandy. Kandy had some magnificent English gardens and the day passed quickly. Then at about 7pm with a full moon casting a surreal mood over the city, we started to hear the snap of whips and soon after here comes the procession of elephants with dancers, more men with whips, more elephants including a magnificent old bull on whose back was the tooth we were all celebrating. We fell in with some Englishmen and moved to their hotel veranda and about 9pm we tried again for a hotel room. Still no luck.

Dottie said she could sleep in a car, so I hired a car to take us on the all- night trip back to Colombo. To my great relief, Dottie weathered the whole experience well and remained healthy. We took some down time in Colombo to make sure Dottie was rested then on to Bombay.

We arrived in India at Bombay and stayed in the Taj Mahal hotel (the scene of a major terrorist attack in the early 21st Century) to give us luxury in what we knew would be an emotionally challenging place. Right call! The very first day we found an English speaking taxi driver who took us to the Tower of Silence where the Zoroastrian tradition put their dead to be devoured by vultures, then to a street where we saw a cobra fight a mongoose to the death (the mongoose won), then to the Red Light district where the woman sold their charms for 10 cents, then to the Ganges River to see the cremation process which ended in the oldest son taking a silver hammer to crack his father's skull as he lay burning to let his soul out of his body.

Perhaps even worse, we went as part of our exploration of India to Calcutta where at the time 500,000 people ate, slept, lived and died on the streets of Calcutta in numbing poverty. Even in the best hotel we could not get away from the smell of urine. Having described these adventures harshly, we were deeply moved by India and the many spiritual traditions it contains and we have been back on our way to Tibet on a climbing trip and were again moved by its exotic and spiritual nature. When I taught at Semester at Sea in 1991 we had a chance to spend another week in India. Wonderful, haunting country.

THE WALK

DOTTIE JOINING ME ON THE WALK

The decision to run for governor was also influenced by the team of talented young people that had formed around the Olympic issue: Tom Nussbaum, John Parr, Meg Lundstrom, Sam Brown, and Howard Gelt, as well as new people like Steve Katich.

I asked my friend Dick Freese to head the campaign, and he took a leave of absence from his law firm of Davis, Graham and Stubbs to do so. Early in 1973 I borrowed a beautiful unit in the Mountain

Haus in Vail, which, along with our house in Vail and Dick and Sigrid Freese's house in Vail, allowed us to sleep the core advisors. What an array of decisions faced us! We knew we had to get a media person in right away. We divided up the tasks: campaign headquarters, furnish the same with equipment, interview media people, finance, and then strong and capable (if young) hands were able to get to work.

It is amazing how a bunch of untested neophytes intuited such a successful campaign. It was magic. Volunteers from the Olympic battle appeared everywhere, dedicated and ready to organize. Fund-raising followed, but we never did raise more than $250,000—a laughably small amount by today's standards. The key to victory, in addition to a dedicated staff, was the walk.

I can't remember who first suggested that I walk the state, but it immediately gained favor with the group. "So Dick Lamm," observed one. It was, it was. I had climbed most of the fourteeners and kayaked a lot of its rivers. I had watched from afar when Lawton Childs had walked in Florida for the US Senate and when Dan Walker did a similar walk for governor of Illinois. Both had gotten elected and credited much of it to the walk.

I hired a very savvy political consultant, Bob Squires, and had a lot of local talent helping me—Olympic veterans Dick and Sigrid Freese, Jim Monaghan, Eric Sondermann, Meg Lundstrom, and Tom Nussbaum among them. Dottie regularly joined us.

So on an early October day in 1973, our whole family caravanned with three or four staff cars to the Colorado–Wyoming line on Highway 87 to start the walk. As predicted, there was incredible press coverage, and I made a little pitch holding my kids. Then off I went. Thirteen miles was scheduled for me to the first farmhouse, where I would spend the night. While I walked, a rotation of my wonderful volunteers would drive ahead another thirteen to fifteen miles and scout out the next family that would house the wandering candidate. I thought thirteen miles would be child's play, but the hard pavement exhausted me at first. The press would come out and interview me by walking a few miles with me, and I made a number of friends among them—which was generally like petting rattlesnakes.

Yes, of course this walk was a campaign gimmick, but it was also a deeply personal journey. I was thirty-eight years old, healthy, happily married, and walking for governor. It was a beautiful fall, and I walked past fields being harvested and through small towns, stopping occasionally to visit a store and say hello. I carried a sign that read "Lamm for Governor" and would salute the cars going by.

The first night I stayed in a farmhouse with a young family—who luckily had some foot-soaking salts. I was sore and stiff but elated at the exercise and being outdoors.

I remember an incredible sense of well-being that first night. A strenuous day of exercise walking among autumn fields and hardworking folk. A wonderful bed with a Colorado farm family. I also had this irrational feeling that the walk was a winning strategy. Sleep, peaceful sleep, soon followed.

It was a very unorthodox way to campaign. I missed many of the Democratic meetings and dinners and most of the chances to speak directly to the party Democrats. My two primary opponents thought I was crazy! "You got to hunt where the ducks are!" said one. But I was communicating with Colorado and loved it. People would come out and meet me and walk the last mile into their town.

There is a paradox in political office where the most important trait of actually serving in office is to learn to say both thank you and no to your friends. I owed so many people who did help elect me and could not help feeling immensely grateful. Many people spent thousands of volunteer hours on my campaign, and I naturally felt and feel grateful. I had interfered with their family life, caused them to lose sleep, and in many cases cost them out of pocket, yet I now had a public trust and a government to run. But to execute your duties of office you must of necessity say no much more often than you say yes. Fiorello LaGuardia once said the hardest thing in politics, but the most important, was to learn to say no to your friends. How true!

Dottie and I have spent a lot of time thinking and discussing this paradox. We decided early on that should lightning strike, our very first party at the mansion was to be for the people I stayed with when I walked the state.

Walking the state was also a strategy born of desperation. I had no money, the regular Democrats were split three ways—with me likely getting the smallest share of the party Democrats—and running even a shoestring campaign was expensive. What to do?

I had come to Colorado because of the outdoors, I was an exercise junkie, and I knew the press would love the image. Richard Nixon at the time was being enveloped by Watergate, and people were cynical and increasingly felt all politicians were crooks. I would just go out and talk with them, stay in their homes, and share a cameo of their lives. The walk was born.

I walked down the Front Range that beautiful fall, watching the leaves turn and the crops get harvested. It was spectacular weather, and I didn't hit even a serious rain until I got to Castle Rock, south of Denver. I stayed with an incredible variety of people, rich and poor. At the end of each day I would tie my red bandanna to a fence post and ride with staff to the family they had selected for that night. In the morning, I would ride back to the bandanna and resume the walk. It turned to be one of the best experiences of my life.

I took from Christmas to May off to attend the legislative session and set off again in May of 1974. I made the Colorado–New Mexico line at Kim, Colorado, and then started to walk through city limits in western Colorado, including Durango, Grand Junction, Alamosa, Pueblo, and more. I also walked from Grand Junction to Delta.

Despite the doubt clouding my choice to campaign this way, my campaign team members were unanimous that we were doing the right thing. As I mentioned, reporters, for both print and TV, would come and walk with me for a morning or even longer. And Dottie was willing and able to represent me at the most important political function—which she did with her usual style and class. We had a live-in babysitter in our basement apartment (the wonderful Lynn Norton), and that gave Dottie some flexibility.

The only downside was that I missed my wife and kids. I would take one day off a week for my family, but it inevitably included some staff meetings. Dick Freese was working his magic, but there were some things that demanded my personal attention.

There was a particular issue that could have scuttled my governor's race, one that added to the stress of my campaign. Shortly after the abortion bill, and while I was inspired by the issue of population, I introduced a bill in the legislature which would limit to two the number of deductions for children taken against the Colorado income tax. I felt that government should not encourage more than two children, and while it didn't have a large economic impact, it was symbolic. But suddenly it dawned how it could be used against me. "Lamm wants to get government involved in the size of your family!" and so on. I held my breath until election day hoping that my two opponents would not do adequate opposition research. They didn't and I escaped, but it taught me to think through the implications of using legislation as a teaching device. Make your speeches and write your op-ed pieces but keep it separate from the legislative process unless you truly want it to pass.

Shortly before the primary, I was named by *Time Magazine* as one of the "Two Hundred Outstanding Young Leaders of America," and I have no doubt this helped in the Democratic primary. I of course did win that primary in September of 1974, but I kept on walking. I completed my journey in late October of 1974, with John Denver walking the last mile beside me in a snowstorm to the state capitol where he gave a free concert. I had walked 888 miles and loved almost every mile and met so many incredible people.

3. GOVERNOR!

OUT OF THE FRYING PAN, INTO THE FIRE

It is scary to think how little career or vocational guidance I got in high school. Virtually none. I had no idea of what occupational goals to pursue. I had no musical talent, no artistic talent, no athletic talent, and no vocational talents, but I did have a strange faith in myself. I took life as a challenge and always rose to the occasion. When we were moving out of the Governor's Mansion in 1987, I found a boyhood newspaper clipping entitled "Today Newspaper Boy," which had my picture and the number of papers I delivered daily (133), and it was captioned, "Wants to Be a CPA." I was twelve years old when this was written and had absolutely no idea what a CPA was, but I so admired my dad who himself had started out as a CPA that it seemed a reasonable answer. I suspect 95 percent of males had little or no idea of what education to pursue, but I was a complete blank. It was only after I was working for a CPA firm in Salt Lake City (1958) that the full enormity of occupational choice settled on me. It did intimidate me a bit, but it also focused my mind. I respond best to challenges.

As Dottie and I had planned, our first party in the Governor's Mansion was for all the families I had stayed with on the walk. Well over one hundred families were invited, and most came. The ornate settings of the Governor's Mansion were intimidating to me, so I can imagine what it was like for a rural farm family or an inner-city family. The state patrol had never seen such an egalitarian event. None of the families knew each other because my having spent the night with each was the only common denominator. I was greeting people at the door, and Dottie came down and heard hearty laughter coming from the Palm Room, the large ornate public room with (at the time) a large flowing fountain in the middle. Dottie investigated and found our three-year-old daughter Heather and her friend Niki, also three, had taken off all their clothes and were splashing in the Palm Room fountain. Dottie called me so I wouldn't miss such a priceless moment, and then we got the little nymphs out of the fountain and on their way to bed. I did wonder what Mrs. Boettcher, Grand Dame of the Denver social scene in the early twentieth century, presidents and senators, statesmen and movies stars, and business leaders and society ladies who had graced the Palm Room would have thought, but I bet none had more fun than our tiny nymphs. Our diverse guests loved it, and it turned out to be the perfect icebreaker.

I took office in January of 1975, and it felt like being hit with a ton of bricks. Moving into the mansion, selling our property (two houses in Denver, our house in Vail, and our twenty-nine acres of land in Evergreen), putting together a cabinet and staff. It was a lot coming at me very fast.

Occasionally I mentally stress that if I would have kept all the property I owned, I would be far better off financially than I am. We sold our two Denver houses at the bottom of the market, and Vail property exploded shortly thereafter as it did in Evergreen. I did not have to sell, but did so out of a feeling that I wanted no distractions and no questions about the "environmental governor" owning mountain land. It didn't work, of course, for soon the *Rocky Mountain News* put a picture of our Vail house on the front page while the story did in fact raise the issue of how an "environmental governor" could own a house in Vail. This was the very issue I was concerned about, so it cost me financially and ended up being a political story after all.

I have always been a highly stressed person, and now I was in a high-stress job. When I had gotten an ulcer during my first year of law school, I learned then to control stress with exercise. And it was now exercise I called upon now to control the stress of governing. I estimate that five days a week I would jog one of the courses I planned out from the Governor's Mansion. Usually late afternoon and usually with my dear friend Arnie Grossman, I would launch myself in one direction or the other. My security people did not want me to run a predictable course or pattern, so we would often have the state patrol take us five miles out,

1OK RUN IN DENVER

and we would then run back to the mansion at Eighth Avenue and Logan Street. I would start the run uptight and uncommunicative and return loose, limber, and stress free. I feel that having that ulcer actually improved my overall health because of my response to it.

In addition, two or three times a week I would have the patrol take me out to Stapleton Plaza in east Denver where my friend John Gillingham had a health club and offered a vigorous aerobics class. The combination of running and aerobics kept me both in good shape and relatively stress free.

A New Cabinet

Choosing a cabinet was wonderful challenge. I enjoyed it and was good at it. I do brag about my ability to spot talent, pick good people, and forge a team. Dick Freese was my right-hand and Sigrid Freese became a very accomplished scheduler and political strategist. I will never be able to repay my debt to the two of them. Then, after six months, Dick Freese came to me and said for the sake of his health, he would have to resign. He had worked day and night for those six months and was exhausted. This was the guy who had put together my campaign and organized the governor's office and helped me on my agenda, and now he was gone. Big, big hole in my life.

I owe Dick Freese a deep debt of gratitude. He was always there when I needed him and he got a lot of grief and stress from our relationship. Dick went to Mexico to recuperate and revitalize. He remained a close advisor, but now I needed a new person to manage the day-to-day operations of the governor's office.

MY INTRODUCTION TO COLORADO

I had participated in ROTC during college, and, after graduating from the University of Wisconsin in 1957 with my second lieutenant bars on my shoulders, I went off to basic officer training camp in Fort Eustis in Williamsburg, Virginia—a lovely, historic town. Basic officer training was rough—lots of long marches, many of them at night. Most of those hikes involved heavy rain.

Halfway through the training, my new friend J. E. Devilbiss and I sneaked off base and drove to the Pentagon in Washington, D.C. In those days, you could just walk right in (we were in uniform)—and success after all is the child of audacity. We found a major who was in charge of assignments, and we asked him to station us at Fort Carson in Colorado upon graduation from Officers School. "Why?" asked the major. "Because we love the mountains," we answered. He laughed. Hardly a military reason, but somehow, we succeeded. He loved our candor and forwardness.

It was during those four months at the end of 1957 when I fell deeply in love with Colorado. J. E. and I would often get up very early to hunt on one of the small ponds on Fort Carson. Then we would give our platoons Physical Training and go to breakfast at the officers club. I earned $225 a month, had a vigorous and healthy lifestyle, and loved

Colorado. Because I had had a year of law school at the University of Wisconsin (I had started law school my senior year of college), I was given legal work to do in my four short months of active duty. I also had a platoon and started to learn how to lead men.

Upon discharge in January of 1958, I went to Aspen to try to become a ski bum. I got a job managing a bunkhouse owned by a guy named Ed Brennen, and I packed ski slopes for ski tickets. A few times I babysat for Ed and his wife's beautiful kids. I learned sometime later that his wife and one of the children had been killed in an auto accident.

Life as a ski bum was too aimless for me, so after a month I packed up and drove to Salt Lake City. Didn't know a soul. Why Salt Lake City? Because it had both a city and skiing. There, I got a job as an accountant for Lincoln G. Kelly, a CPA firm, doing tax work. I found a quaint basement apartment at 435 E. First South (how can you forget an address like that?), met a wonderful young lady named Sue Lewin, and enjoyed Salt Lake City immensely. I loved to ski, but I had to be productive in some way and could not live the life of a ski bum—even in Aspen. Good trait or bad, that is my reality.

THE GOVERNORSHIP

I have a strange reluctance to write about the governorship. Obviously, it was my occupational high point, but it also contained many bitter moments and memories. Dottie's cancer, some political defeats, twelve years of being on call 24-7. Bittersweet.

I remember the first time I entered the Governor's Mansion in 1967 at a reception for the state legislators. Fun and interesting, but I had no thoughts that we would someday live there. With small children at home, Dottie and I missed most lobbyist parties for state legislators, but we never missed the governor's reception for the legislators. We attended eight of them. The first was in 1967, where I was a new entity; at the second in 1968, I was a hero to many because of the abortion bill but was also snubbed by a few. Governor John Love was always welcoming, as was his wife, Ann, who sincerely (if quietly) congratulated me on the abortion bill.

After the 1974 election, Governor John Vanderhoof couldn't have been more helpful in our transition, although one could tell he was hurt and didn't really understand how Colorado could have elected a thirty-nine-year-old environmentalist.

What did happen in Colorado in the early 1970s? When I asked Senator Gary Hart in the summer of 2017, he treated it as a stupid question. "All the new people like you and me!" he offered. Yes, clearly that was part of it, but don't forget a Watergate year, the walk, the Olympics. Congressional candidates Pat Schroeder and Craig Barnes plowing the ground for the rest of us. Some mix of these certainly accounted for a lot of the victory. Could I have won with two of the three? Probably, but who knows?

Not being born in Colorado has never come up as an issue in my career. Colorado is a very welcoming state. In fact, we did not have a governor who was born in Colorado until the mid-1930s. We are the land of hope to many transplants. Run the list: I was born in Wisconsin, Senator Tim Wirth in New Mexico, Senator Gary Hart in Kansas, Senator Bill Armstrong in Nebraska, Representative Pat Schroeder in Oregon, Governor Bill Owens in Texas, Governor John Hickenlooper in Pennsylvania, and so on.

Looking back on these times, it seems more obvious than it did when we were in the middle of it. Colorado was blessed in the 1960s and the 1970s with a constant stream of young adults looking for jobs and a good quality of life. Because of the Vietnam War, they were increasingly politicized, and Earth Day in April of 1970 further galvanized young newcomers. But the war and the ensuing draft hung over America like a Sword of Damocles. Denver lawyer Craig Barnes first tapped into it in Colorado when he challenged Bryon Rogers, a traditional pro–Lyndon Johnson Democrat. Pat Schroeder filled the Congressional seat in 1974 in the same election that voted out the Olympics. On the surface, political pundits considered Colorado to be a red state, but something dramatic had changed. The 1974 election was a hinge election. Colorado was now a purple state with a growing pro-environment antiwar Democratic Party, fueled by a legion of active young people. The political winds had shifted. Big time, as it turned out.

I was elected governor at thirty-nine and had never run anything larger than a small law office. I had been preceded by twelve years of Republican governors, and I had deeply offended many business people by opposing the Olympics as well as a significant number of people by my sponsorship of liberalized abortion. Being governor is a sink-or-swim job, and no sooner had I taken office when I started to sink. Most of my problems were self-imposed, as I struggled with all the was required in my new role, and tried to be a husband and father to two small kids. Politically, I could seem to do nothing right.

Moving into the Governor's Mansion was a family project. No more twin sinks in the master bedroom, which we had built into 2500 South Logan Street. Now we each had our own bathroom—Dottie's with ceiling-to-floor mirrors, 360°. (A legacy of Mrs. Boettcher.) I suggested that she take bread crumbs so she could find her way out.

The kids both had their own bedroom and Scott soon moved to the third-floor bedroom that had been the maid's quarters, which suited Scott well. Our children's reactions to the experience was dramatically opposite. Heather took to the lifestyle like Eloise at the Ritz. She made friends with the changing cast of mansion employees and state patrol officers (at least one stationed at the mansion at all times), but Scott didn't like the opulent quarters we were living in and especially didn't like living with security and all that entailed. Scott is a born egalitarian.

One of my few regrets in a life filled with accomplishment is how my lifestyle weighed on Scott. Dottie tells the story of Scott's mediocre grades and his justification that he just wanted to be "average." At the utterance of these words, Dottie was off to Colorado Academy in southwest Denver, observing,

FAMILY CHRISTMAS, 1975

"If Scott wants 'just to be average,' we are going to get him into a school where 'average' will be the 'high.' Scott got along well at Colorado Academy, but by tenth grade, he wanted to go to East High School in Denver. We granted his wish reluctantly, but Scott did well at East and played lacrosse with a good and interesting bunch of diverse friends. He has turned out to be a wonderful, and still egalitarian human being.

In our last year in the mansion we invited both Scott's and Heather's favorite teachers to the Governor's Mansion to say thank you for their good work. Ever after I would always tell a teacher, "Thank you for being a teacher." I do so to this day.

At some-point midway through my service I got an artist to design and produce a little metal figurine. Every month we would have a teacher of the month, and every year we would have all the nominated teachers to a reception at the Governor's Mansion and would give them a figurine. I would inevitably recount to the assembled teachers how Dottie and I knew our teachers were underpaid and underrecognized, and I would quote Napoleon on the need to recognize excellence: "I can get men to die for little pieces of ribbon." I didn't want them to die, of course, but I wanted a symbol of Colorado's gratitude for their good efforts, and was honoring them for being dedicated teachers.

We did very little entertaining in the mansion (we didn't have the money), but every year we would throw two or three little Christmas parties for friends and supporters. The mansion would sprout Christmas trees, wreaths, and greens, and at the appointed hour, some three hundred guests. These parties were built into the Governor's Mansion budget—probably because we always invited the legislators and their spouses. The legislature was always parsimonious with the mansion budget and we were constantly underfunded, but they always came through on the three Christmas parties.

IN OFFICE

My first year was a disaster. I couldn't do anything right—and it was mostly my fault. My staff was loyal, always hard-working, but often glum that first year. They handled critical telephone calls and acquainted themselves with the business of government, but a dark cloud hung over the whole office. I was the cause of that black cloud. Bumper stickers appeared on the streets that referred back to my campaign: "Lamm Could Walk the State, But Can't Run It." But, slowly I learned the ropes, the mood improved, and soon the whole wonderful staff sparkled with dedication and purpose.

The year 1975 was a difficult time to hold office all over the country. Watergate had given the press new status and power. They had been indispensable in exposing Richard Nixon, and so many reporters wanted to be investigative reporters. I could not meet with my leadership for breakfast without one or two reporters hanging over the table. Everybody recognized that it was a new era but no one knew the rules. But most of the fault was mine.

I am proud of the people I brought into office; it is the one thing I brag about. Lots of wonderful young people who went on to success and made great contributions to the Colorado community. Ditto my cabinet members. We had productive and (usually) spirited cabinet meetings and some wonderful retreats at various locations in the Colorado mountains. When the inevitable question comes, "What is your proudest accomplishment?" I always answer, "We ran the state honestly and well." And we did! Second answer is the people we brought into state government and gave a start on their careers.

LIVING WITH SECURITY

Living with security was a difficult matter for me. There was a whole range of wonderful young men whose job was to protect and take a bullet for me if necessary. They were with me a majority of each week and were on duty at night when I slept. I loved the individuals, but still resented an incredible imposition on privacy.

Shortly after I took office, Dottie and I decided to climb a mountain in Estes Park, north of Denver. My chief of security insisted that I take a long a security officer. I had not yet recognized that it was I who was boss, not them, but I knew if anything happened to me they would be blamed for not protecting me. We had a wonderful day, and our only danger was getting the security officer off the mountain. He could bench press four hundred pounds, but he had had no climbing experience.

In the early 1980s I decided to take my son, Scott, on an adventure trip running a wild river in Peru. Consternation! How many security officers would this take? Peru was at the time in the midst of some serious unrest, involving Maoist guerillas who called themselves Shining Path.

None, I informed the patrol, we were going alone. The state patrol, ever vigilant, looked at the trip and found in addition to the danger of the river, that we had to go through territory controlled by the Shining Path guerrillas. More consternation, but this time I took it more seriously. We booked the trip without hint of my office, and off we went, leaving at the gate a confident wife/mother and two worried-looking state patrol officers.

The trip was terrific! Not a lot of dangerous water but always enough to be interesting. Our guide had asked me before I left if I could bring twelve copies of *Playboy* magazine. "Trust me," said the guide, when I raised an eyebrow.

We flew to a town near the river where we all packed into a Land Rover. It took a day and a half to get to the put-in point of the river, and the need for *Playboy*s soon became apparent. Not far into this leg of the journey we were stopped by men in uniforms with guns to check our papers. One *Playboy* expedited the clearance. We were stopped at a number of additional checkpoints, sometimes by people without uniforms, but a *Playboy* always got us through. At the end of the trip our guide did tell me that some of the checkpoints were controlled by "intruders." There was no trouble, and to this day I don't know the extent of the risk we were running. As I look back on it, it was unwise to risk my son and my office on such a trip. And while we got away with it, I didn't make it a practice.

To some extent, I wanted to continue to live the same kind of life that we lived before office. I was not willing to give up everything. I would often drive the whole family up to the mountains to ski or hike, and one time I drove the whole family after a governor's conference in New Jersey down the East Coast to my parents' home in Naples, Florida. It was a great family bonding trip and the type of thing Dottie and I instinctively knew was important to our kids at their ages.

On another occasion, I drove the governor's car on a quiet Sunday night down to the Denver Athletic Club to pick up my daughter, Heather, and a friend. While stopped at a stoplight, a drunk driver came along and swerved into four or five cars, causing serious damage. I turned on the siren and the red lights recessed in the car's grille,

CROSS COUNTRY SKI RACE, 1976

and the guy stopped. What to do now? I got on the radio to the mansion, and soon the Denver Police arrived, but again I was nicely told by the state patrol that I should not have stopped the guy. This time I think I was right as this drunk was going to hurt someone before long. Turns out that he was an illegal alien and the police let him go the following morning when he was sober. So much for immigration laws and so much for laws against drunk driving!

But I doff my cap to the Colorado State Patrol. Cautious, courageous, courteous, they were wonderful, and our family and the state owe them a lot. We ran into some resistance when we hired a woman as a regular patrol officer, but she was out on patrol only a month into her job when she took down a large, drunk man who outweighed her by a hundred pounds. Most of the opposition stopped.

LIEUTENANT GOVERNOR GEORGE BROWN

The Democratic Party picks the lieutenant governor candidate, not the gubernatorial candidate, thank you very much! It is a carefully guarded prerogative. At the 1974 state assembly/convention they picked senator George Brown, a Black state senator who had an honorable career and was a gifted orator. Of the four best speeches I'd heard in my eight years in the Colorado legislature, George Brown made three of them (including one the day after Martin Luther King Jr. was assassinated). I liked and admired George, but we had a hard time working together, especially at a staff level. Lieutenant governors always want, and often deserve, more duties than the constitution gives them. And with us, I am willing to admit the fault might be mine. There was conflict inherent built into the relationship.

Due to my insensitive handling of the issue, I was not even inaugurated before I had a conflict with the lieutenant governor (elect) and the Black legislative leadership. I had committed to having an African American cabinet member, but when it came to satisfying all the constituencies of the Democratic Party, there was simply not enough positions. I felt that with

George as my lieutenant governor, my pledge was fulfilled. Not according to soon-to-be Mayor and First Lady Wellington and Wilma Webb, however; George had won the position on his own, and I had an outstanding obligation.

It was an obligation that I normally would have taken a great deal of pleasure in fulfilling, but I was balancing all the interests that were pressing in on me; I tried to make George serve two roles, and he had won one on his own. My mistake. Wellington and Wilma Webb and others picketed my inauguration and continued their pressure—all within the rules of politics, and they burned no bridges. Finally, I got the message and made the appointment. Thereafter, the relationship between the two offices was cordial but tense.

George was one of two Black lieutenant governors elected that year—the first two since Reconstruction. He did have some minor duties given to the lieutenant governor by the Colorado Constitution, but it was not enough for a smart, vital man.

One day while I was out of state at a governor's conference, George pardoned Sylvester Lee Garrison, a Black man convicted of murder who had spent some time on death row. George claimed Mr. Garrison had not received a fair trial because he was a Black man convicted by an all-white jury. No other mitigating circumstances. I looked into the case when I returned and did not think there were any valid grounds for clemency, and I revoked the pardon. After that, we maintained communication, but barely.

George decided not to run for reelection and went on to be an executive at Grumman Corporation. Looking back on these years, I see that I was at fault for not creating a more vital role for both my lieutenant governors. George was invited to all our cabinet meetings and retreats but seldom came. He was a good but flawed man. As am I.

A word about Lieutenant Governor Nancy Dick. She won a primary also and became my lieutenant governor in 1978. A smart and effective legislator, Nancy made a number of new roles for herself. A lovely woman who had lost her husband years before in an automobile accident when they had small kids, she earned the family living, raised her children, and found time to be a real civic contributor in Pitkin County. I am again at fault at not devising enough to really challenge her talents, but what is past is past. Life happens to you when you are busy making other plans, and there are no reruns.

THE ONE-ROOM SCHOOLHOUSE

In 1942, my family had moved from Arlington Heights, Illinois, to a rural community called Biltmore outside of Barrington, Illinois. We lived in a beautiful white house on a corner with a large backyard and a stream flowing in a gully on what must have been part of our property line. Our new house would be an impressive dwelling even by today's standards; Dad was clearly on the fast track in his company. Biltmore was at the end of the Northwestern Railroad in Barrington plus about a ten-mile drive, which my father undertook every weekday despite gas rationing. As secretary/treasurer for United Electric, he obviously thought the long commute to downtown Chicago—probably an hour and a half each way—was worthwhile to give his family an idyllic surrounding. There were large areas of forest in our immediate neighborhood with paths connecting the houses of other neighborhood kids, where we would fight out World War II with toy guns.

My local school in Biltmore was a one-room schoolhouse presided over by a Mrs. Reed, whose first name is lost to history. All eight grades were in one room, accompanied by a coal stove to keep us warm and the creative dedication of Mrs. Reed, whom I suspect earned less than $500 a year. Mrs. Reed knew how to keep us all busy; there were our studies, our art projects, making potholders from some bright string, dividing into two groups of roughly equivalent age groups for a spelling bee, and identifying places on the world globe. In fourth grade I was the smartest kid in my class, an honor undiminished by the fact that I was the only kid in fourth grade. Talent won out.

We had about thirty kids in grades one through eight, and everyone got along and because we didn't know anything different; we accepted this arrangement as the way all schools were organized.

Nothing clued us in to the fact that we were an unusual school until our softball team started to play neighboring schools. There were not enough agile sixth-, seventh-, or eighth-grade boys in our school to field a softball team, so we recruited a couple of girls. While we played among ourselves this seemed a small thing, but once we visited a neighboring and larger school we got immediately mocked for having such "misconstructed" team members. This was, after all, the 1940s. The fact that the two girls on our team were better than most of the rest of us didn't save us the indignity of having to play the game with these fellow students, which rumor had it, were missing important body parts.

I had an idyllic childhood, and I do realize how lucky I was. Loving parents who took a great interest in their children and who had the resources to meet all their needs and then some. The one-room school had its drawbacks but also its great assets. We were a community committed to each other. Memories of spellings bees in in that schoolhouse surface, and how proud I was in fifth grade when my brother Tom joined us in first grade. My first fight was in that schoolyard, and it was there at home plate where I had my nose broken by a tipped ball. It was softball, but still no one ever suggested I get a catcher's mask. One-room schoolhouses don't have money for such things in their budget.

LAMM TO ELDERLY: DROP DEAD

During my time as governor, there were several big issues that I grappled with, and that again landed me in the middle of controversy. One in particular, was, of course, my stance on health care.

It was a sleepy spring afternoon in March of 1984, and I was in my third term as governor of Colorado. I was in a small meeting of health lawyers in the back room of a Denver hospital, when I took exception to the term "right to die" used by my a questioner. I observed that death is not an option and that instead "we have a duty to die." To be precise, here are the words transcribed from my press secretary's tape recorder:

The real question gets into, then, high technology medicine. Every year in the United States we have a million and a half heart attacks. Six hundred thousand of them die. How many Barney Clarks can we afford? How many heart transplants can we afford?

You know, we at least ought to be talking about that. I think that we're rapidly approaching the day where medical science can keep people alive in hospitals, hooked up to tubes and things, far beyond when any kind of quality of life is left at all. But yet medical science can keep us alive.

It seems to be that it's at least a question society ought to be talking about, what are the ethical implications?

A terrific article that I've read, one of the philosophers of our time, I think, is a guy named Leon Kiss—has anybody seen his stuff? He's just terrific. In *The American Scholar* last year he wrote an article called "The Case for Mortality," where essentially he said we have a duty to die. It's like if leaves fall off a tree forming the humus for the other plants to grow out. We've got a duty to die and get out of the way with all of our machines and artificial hearts and everything else like that and let the other society, our kids, build a reasonable life.

(Tape provided courtesy of the *Denver Post*.)

When we left the meeting, I asked Sue O'Brien, my excellent and savvy press secretary, if there would be any news coming out of the event. "I doubt it," ventured O'Brien, who would spend ten hours a day for the next three weeks putting out fires we had just unwittingly ignited.

The next morning, I arose at four thirty, as is my wont, and worked on a book I was soon to publish. At seven a.m. I came down in my running clothes and asked the state patrol officer to open up the security gates. I was aware of the distant ringing of many phones. "Governor, don't you want to see the newspapers?" asked the officer. "Thanks, no. I'll read them later," I responded.

I walked out into the front yard of the governor's residence and got halfway to the automatic gates, which were lumbering open, when it struck me that the patrolman on duty, who had become a friend of the family (as is always the case for people with whom you share a significant part of your) looked worried. It was clearly not like him to ask me if I wanted the paper when I was on my way to run. I returned and asked for the paper.

There on the front page of the *Denver Post*, right below the fold, was the story, "Gov. Lamm Says Elderly and Terminally Ill Have Duty to Die." He then handed me a thick stack of phone messages on a spindle. Political death seemed near—I felt I was reading my obituary.

Besides the predictable press calls were an array of citizen calls (we kept the governor's residence listed in the phone book), ranging from support to threats. One caller urged me to get tested for Alzheimer's disease, a diagnosis he said he had long suspected for me.

You cannot imagine the shock wave that hits a governor's office when there is a crisis like this. One of the joys of being governor is that your staff are so much more than employees; they work long and hard hours out of a mixture of dedication, ideology, and camaraderie that makes them more a team than a staff.

The team often seems to mirror the mood and fortunes of the governor. When things go well, the team has a wonderful esprit de corps. Jealousies are present but minimized. The mood has the buoyancy of a group who knows it is doing important and valuable work. The climate is sunny. But my governorship had been through storms. Ten years later, it looked like those terrible times of my first year were coming back.

Sue O'Brien greeted me at the office with an invitation to *Good Morning America* and a bushel basket of press inquiries. My chief of staff had been getting calls from Democratic legislators and party officials. My administrative assistant was juggling an incessantly ringing telephone, and my security people seemed especially attentive lest some octogenarian might pummel me with a cane.

Coincidentally, a group of Colorado senior citizens was meeting at a church across from the capitol. My staff quickly arranged an appearance, and by eleven a.m., with a flock of TV cameras and press, we walked across the street. I asked myself, "After trying mightily to get press interest in some of Colorado's most serious problems, how could a few thoughtful words cause this much commotion?

I was put immediately at ease by a warm reception and had a meaningful dialogue with thoughtful seniors. The chairman tried to help me off the hook: Did I mean "right to die"? "No," I responded. "Death is not an option or a right, but the fate of all of us." And so it went for an hour.

That morning I started hearing a theme, which, surprisingly, I kept hearing. A large number of seniors believed that they did have a "duty to die." On the way out, one lady handed me a piece of paper with a quote she said Thomas Jefferson wrote to John Adams as both neared death. "It is reasonable that we should drop off and make room for another growth. When we have lived our generation out, we should not wish to encroach upon another."

That theme kept coming up during the following weeks. A significant minority of the letters we received believed in the misquote and told me not to back down. I have come to agree with it, but now, as a senior citizen myself; I have the bona fides to venture an opinion of a group I am myself in. I stand pat.

Two days after the article appeared, I was on the *Today Show* and a number of other national programs. Three days later President Ronald Reagan was asked in a press conference whether he agreed with Governor Lamm that seniors had a "duty to die." To his great credit he responded that he understood that that wasn't exactly what was said. I really appreciated his fairness.

Slowly, the news tide ebbed and life returned to normal. Hundreds of editorials were written, columnists praised and blamed, and one newspaper titled its article, "Lamm to Elderly: Drop Dead."

I learned several lessons from this experience: First, the press overall is committed to truth and free inquiry. The *Denver Post*, while never admitting it was in error, did "clarify" my remarks and wrote a laudatory editorial saying wasn't it wonderful to have a thoughtful and provocative governor. Second lesson was that America was ripe to have a dialogue on death and dying. Within a few years most states (today all fifty) have living will legislation or the equivalent. Third was that if you are sincere and don't back down, the public will admire a certain level of candid outspokenness. Both while in office and after, a large number of people have come up to me and said something to the effect of, "I don't always agree with you, but I sure admire you for speaking out forcefully and candidly."

The fourth lesson is not so positive: politicians should stay away from sensitive subjects. You can understand why politicians tend to be prosaic and boring. Science advances when a scientist states a new truth, inviting and welcoming criticism and correction. Truth advances by the yin and yang of argument. But in politics, every new idea, every new program proposed, and even every new word and phrase risks uncontrollable controversy and defeat. None of the "feedback" loop that science is built upon can be counted on in politics because, if you give your opponent an opening, you risk political death. Even though the polls showed I suffered no damage from the misquote, the obvious message to the political establishment was "stay safe and boring." But I took the opposite lesson. I became ever more aware that I had good instincts and foresight. There are often issues our there that are ripe for change and await the audacious spokesperson.

4. BEYOND THE GOVERNOR

RISK-TAKER

Very uncoordinated and awkward, I was not an athlete in high school. Instead, I was a perfect "late bloomer." Although from age twenty-one on I kept myself in good shape, in high school I wasn't even close to the gold standard of status—a football player or athlete in some other sport. In fact, I had no musical talent, no artistic talent, no athletic talent, and was definitely an introvert. I had no easy talent for talking to girls. I longed to distinguish myself in some way. I chose adventure.

In the summer between tenth and eleventh grades, I applied to be a bellboy in Atlantic City and was accepted. I proudly told my parents and my mother immediately vetoed the idea. There was talk of loose women and bad influences, which didn't sound so bad to me. Nothing I could do would change her mind, though. My dad, who had a hardscrabble upbringing, was indifferent but deferred to my mother. I turned down the offer.

Meanwhile, I had heard of the Pittsburgh Fishing Club in northern Ontario, a resort of people mainly from Pittsburgh. I applied as a waiter and was accepted. In mid-June I flew to Ontario, Canada, where I was joined by three other new employees. We were then picked up in a sea plane and flown to the club over endless miles of verdant forest and picturesque lakes.

The resort had a rotating two hundred guests, and we served them three meals a day, and a group of local Indians did most of the dishes.

The guys slept in a bunkhouse, and we had some rotation that allowed us time off for fishing. I even took an overnight solo fishing trip in a canoe—sleeping under a full moon. Big step for a seventeen-year-old—reading maps and paddling a long way and setting up a lonely overnight camp under a breathtakingly beautiful full moon. The first of many memorable summers, and the first step in making me a man and a risk-taker.

One day, we killed a rattlesnake right outside our wooden cabin and threw it under the bunkhouse. On one of following nights, dressed in my swimming suit and moccasins, I walked out of our bunkhouse to take an evening swim. I had only hit the first step when I heard an ominous rattle right below me. I must have set the broad-jump record as I leaped over the snake. Scared me to death. I was told by one of our guests that my snake was likely the mate of the one we had killed. I decided then and there never to kill snakes gratuitously, and I have kept to that pledge ever since, despite a number of opportunities. Life in the outdoors gives you some opportunities to do so, but for the last forty years I have not wanted to kill any wild thing. While governor, I did kill a beautiful deer with magnificent antlers on my one real hunting trip back into the mountains. But no more.

After high school, I attended summer school at the University of Wisconsin. At one point, I hitchhiked from Madison, Wisconsin, to Lancaster, Ohio, and found myself one late and rainy night dropped off at a seemingly deserted crossroads. I was very concerned (scared, really) until along came a car—the only car I saw that night—after I'd already spent a full hour in the rain. The driver stopped and took me to an all-night diner, where I talked a trucker into a ride home to Pittsburgh. Ended up getting there almost as fast as if I had flown. And all the time, maturing, rising to challenges, learning that life eventually takes care of you. Learning to be audacious. Learning how to be a man.

After my first year in college, I got a job as a deckhand on an ore boat plying the Great Lakes. Wow, college freshman bunking with seasoned sailors! Learning how to get in a harness and being hoisted over to the dock so I could secure our boat to one of the four giant cables that held it to the loading dock. But mostly boring work: chipping paint, endlessly chipping paint.

Lord, did I get lonesome on that boat. At night under a full moon I thought of my high school friends partying and having the summer of their lives while I was sitting on some distant ore boat, lonesome and a little bit homesick. But all the time, I was accumulating different experiences, learning to make my way in the world. Learning to be a risk-taker.

The summer between my sophomore and junior year, my dad helped get me a job in a lumber camp in Elkton, Oregon. I took one of the early train dome cars on a three-day trip cross country—one night in the dome car under a full moon—reading Thomas Wolfe and his lust for life. There was a memorable passage I would keep going back to, where Wolfe describes being on the platform of the last car of a train going through Virginia, under a full moon, on his way home to Ashville, North Carolina. He describes how he wanted to read every book, eat every meal, drink every drink, sleep with every woman—this immense vomit of words, tingling with energy and passion. It's still on my shelf so I take it down and read it again at age eighty. Not great literature but still pulsing with energy.

I took a room in a former motel in Elkton, Oregon; bought a hot plate; and went to work for the Snellstrom Lumber Company. My first assignment was "pulling green chain," where I would pull the lumber off the conveyer after it was cut by a large and dangerous saw and store the wood in piles. Left me exhausted after a day and so sore I could hardly move.

After a week of this initiation, and I was transferred to the woods to build logging roads and became somewhat skilled at putting in cattle guards as well. I hated to see those beautiful Douglas firs fall—dozens a day in just our sector. Broke my heart in fact, but I had committed for a summer. Still, my feeling of loss for the trees we were cutting down did not prevent the summer from being a great experience.

One of the workers on the road crew was a lad just a little older than I was, and he befriended me because he was curious about my life and we could discuss books. It was my first mentoring role, and I relished assigning him books to read and ideas to explore. He and his girlfriend took me on weekends up and down the coast of Oregon, hiking on trails and along the seashore. We had a great time, and as I was leaving at the end of the summer he told me that I was "the best friend he ever had," which made me feel wretched because it showed how few educated people he had ever met and foreshadowed his likely prosaic future. But perhaps that's too pessimistic and judgmental—perhaps, but likely he lived out his class destiny. I figured that my dad was much like him: born to an economically challenged family. But my dad had drive and purpose. I would love to know what became of him, because he did have potential, and I tried to help him see his potential.

At the end of summer, I hitchhiked down to San Francisco to meet my parents and brothers who were on a road trip, and the five of us drove home to Ohio, but not before going through Colorado. My first Colorado experience. Little did I know.

VAIL, 1980

Colorado swore in Roy Romer as its forty-third governor in January of 1987. That very night, the state patrol took us to the airport, and we soon were ensconced in the Montgomery House on Occom Pond in Hanover, New Hampshire. I had been appointed Montgomery Fellow at Dartmouth College for the winter and spring quarters. The Montgomery House was the best house we ever lived in—better even than the Governor's Mansion. Our lawn sloped down to Occom Pond, and the house sported plenty of room for studies, bedrooms for visiting kids, and was a wonderful place for entertaining. It was the perfect transition; wonderful students in an idyllic surrounding. Dottie and I taught and audited classes, went cross-country skiing among the maple trees, and both fell in love with Dartmouth and Hanover. We ended up spending almost a year at Dartmouth and loved every minute of it. They seemed to love us as well, for in 1995 they invited Dottie to be the Montgomery Fellow! It was there that I fully realized what I had missed in not getting a full liberal arts education. To this day, I have more spirit and loyalty to Dartmouth than any place I ever attended or taught.

In the summer of 1987 I accepted a teaching position in Innsbruck, Austria, partly because our dear friends Steve and Moira Ambrose were teaching there also. We had a lovely little apartment in the hills above Innsbruck. It was a wonderful summer teaching, hiking, and sightseeing.

FIFTY YEARS OF FRIENDSHIP

Judy Dorlester was to become an important person in my life. Judy wanted to meet me because she was headed off that fall to my college, the University of Wisconsin. I saw Judy two or three times that summer in various contexts, and when I returned to Madison that fall I looked her up. Judy was seventeen years old, a precocious and already beautiful woman, mature beyond her years.

Back in Madison, I invited Judy to a party we were giving in our apartment above the pub and introduced her to my roommate, Steve Ambrose. Spontaneous combustion: I had never seen a couple fall in love in an instant. Soon I was vacating the apartment two afternoons a week while love bloomed. One year later when Steve and Judy got married, *McCall's Magazine* ran a cover story on them as an ideal American couple.

Steve and Judy Ambrose turned out to be my lifelong friends, but tragically measured in their too-short lives. Upon graduation Steve stayed at the university and got a PhD in history and went on to become one of America's famous historians. (*D-Day, Band of Brothers, Undaunted Courage*).

My future wife, Dottie, and I had barely started dating when we visited Steve and Judy in New Orleans, followed by a couple of more visits where we got to see their two lovely children. Steve rose quickly in the academic ranks and taught very popular courses at Louisiana State University. One night in 1999 we were devastated to receive the news that Judy had committed suicide. A tragic end to a wonderful love story. Brilliant, beautiful, two wonderful children, but...

But I cannot yet leave Steve Ambrose. He was such an important part of my early life. I met him when we were both rushing Chi Psi Fraternity at the University of Wisconsin. Even though he was playing football for the university, he had a cigarette between his lips. We roomed together during my first and last year of college. We kept in touch over the years, and he always had the cigarette. Steve knew they were bad for him, but he couldn't or wouldn't stop. Much later, we went fishing in Alaska and amidst some of the world's best trout fishing, Steve would have to stop for a cigarette.

When in the mid-1960s Steve was teaching in Baton Rouge, he got a phone call, and a female voice said, "The president would like to speak to you." Steve naturally assumed it was the president of LSU but the next voice on the line was Dwight D. Eisenhower. Ike had read one of Steve's books on the Civil War, was impressed with it, and asked Steve to be his biographer. Steve said yes and devoted years to the project.

Judy died leaving Steve with two young kids, and soon Moira, another wonderful woman, appeared on the scene. She lived nearby and suddenly appeared to help Steve with his children, and after a while, moved in. Steve was lost without Judy, but gradually recovered, and over the next year, fell in love with Moira.

The summer of 1987, fresh off the political treadmill, and after a magical winter and spring at Dartmouth, Dottie and I went to Innsbruck, Austria where I taught for a wonderful summer at the University of New Orleans at Innsbruck, Austria. One attraction of this appointment is that Steve was also teaching there. That summer we had bought a new Volvo with which we explored Europe and did some great hiking. We could leave from our apartment on foot and be in the mountains in 15 minutes for some wonderful local hiking.

One of Steve's books was *Pegasus Bridge*, the story of the first Allies on the ground on June 6, 1944. Pegasus Bridge was a key bridge that needed to be taken and held to prevent German reinforcements from reaching Normandy beach. In June 1987, my wife, Dottie, and I, along with Steve and Moria, had dinner in Innsbruck, Austria, with both the English colonel who had commanded the glider attack and the German officer who had commanded the German troops guarding the bridge. Steve had brought these two old foes together earlier, and they had bonded and were available to Steve when Steve had students in Europe. Magical evening for history buffs.

Dottie and I had also traveled with Steve and Moira to Europe during the summer of 1984, where we toured Europe's various battlefields. What a privilege to be at the fortieth anniversary of D-Day (where Steve spent two hours with Tom Brokaw of NBC recounting the D-Day landing) or visiting Verdun or Waterloo or Potsdam with a military historian. We were also with Steve for a week in Montana as he followed the Lewis and Clark Trail in preparation for *Undaunted Courage*. I was also with Steve on a train trip from Omaha, Nebraska, to Reno, Nevada, as he was researching *Nothing Like It in the World: The Men Who Built the Transcontinental Railroad, 1863–1869*. The train was put at Steve's disposal along with some vintage Pullman cars where we slept and ate in luxury. Our mutual love of history was always a great part of our bonding.

I was shattered when one night in Colorado I received a phone call from Steve informing me that he had been diagnosed with lung cancer. We stayed with them one last time in New Orleans in 2002, where Steve and his son Hugh proudly showed us the National WWII Museum that Steve initiated, organized, and inspired. It is now among the most visited places in New Orleans.

The four of us were guests of Tom Brokaw at his ranch in Montana one wonderful week in the early 1990s. The Brokaws loved history and admired Steve and his writing.

Dottie and I visited Steve and Moira at the end of our trip around the world with Semester at Sea. We saw Steve briefly at the hospital and were scheduled to go back the next day for a longer visit when we got an early morning telephone call that Steve had died. Age sixty-six. Tom Hanks and Steven Spielberg flew in for the wake/memorial, and we said good-bye to my dearest friend. Football player, remarkable historian, father, friend for fifty years. *National Geographic* captures him perfectly:

> Ambrose was an Explorer-in-Residence for the National Geographic Society. For him, teaching and writing were two sides of the same coin. "In each case I am telling a story—I think of myself as sitting around the campfire after a day on the trail, telling stories that I hope will have the members of the audience, or the readers, leaning forward just a bit, wanting to know what happens next."

I can affirm his method of research. When we joined Steve in Montana to follow the Lewis and Clark Trail, Steve made us all get out of our canoes at one point and push them upstream for a couple of hundred yards to get to know what it was like for the explorers. "If you seek his monument," go the National WWII Museum in New Orleans. It simply would not have been there without Steve Ambrose.

The outdoors has been an indispensable part of my life. I have climbed fifty of Colorado's fifty-four 14,000-foot mountains as well as Mount Whitney in California and Mount Fuji in Japan, and I have kayaked or rafted many of the rivers in the West, including the Grand Canyon on a wonderful ten-day trip. When I was in law school, I went to Zion National Park and spent three days walking the Virgin River, a wild river bordered by magnificent walls that extend upward thousands of feet. The canyon is very narrow, and when hikers get caught by a rainstorm, they are in deep trouble. I was on one fatal climb on Little Bear Peak in Colorado, when one of our party was going too fast on a knife ridge and fell. I literally ran down the mountain to get help while the rest of the party rescued and stabilized him, but by the time the helicopter arrived he had died. It was incredibly sobering and tragic.

Once out of office, I was able to take speaking opportunities. I essentially put both my kids through private colleges with my speaking income.

The great benefit of the "Duty to Die" episode was that it made me a national spokesperson of sorts for end-of-life issues and health care. I spoke at annual dinners of hospitals, nurses' and doctors' conventions, and I was even invited to speak to the American Medical Association. It was wonderful getting paid for something I loved doing. I also wrote a book, *The Brave New World of Health Care*, after leaving office, which was very well received by the people who read it. It was of course controversial, by the public policy framework. The following is taken from that book, as well as my follow-up, *The Brave New World of Healthcare Revisited*, published in 2003 and 2013, respectively.

THE SOMETIME CRUELTY OF COMPASSION

Once again paraphrasing economist Kenneth Boulding, one of the basic dilemmas of public policy is that all of our policy experience deals with the past, and all our decisions relate to the future. These policy decisions will be exacerbated by the very successes of our past. The incredible bounty of the interaction between a sparsely populated continent filled with abundant resources and an energetic people has masked the need for making hard choices. It has allowed us to fool ourselves that we can satisfy more desires and expectations than we realistically can afford.

Public policy is too often driven by identified needs and identified individuals to the exclusion of other public goods. One of the great challenges of the twenty-first century will be to learn the wisdom of George Bernard Shaw's aphorism: "The mark of a truly educated man is to be truly moved by statistics." Public policy is burdened by the difficulty of making unidentified lives equal to identified lives. Statistics often represent people not numbers. But, as a nun once told me, "Statistics are people with the tears washed off."

Professor Alan Wertheimer raises the following provocative questions: Suppose the following were true, he asks:

> At least some of the money spent on open-heart surgery could be used to prevent heart disease. True, patients in need of such surgery might die, but many more lives would be saved.
>
> Some money spent treating tooth decay among low-income children might be used on fluoridation and dental hygiene. True, some decay would go untreated, but fewer children would ever need such treatment.
>
> (Wertheimer 1980)

He points out "all involve choosing between a policy designed to help specific persons and one that seeks to prevent the need for such help." These choices are especially difficult because we know who need the help. "We must often choose between helping identifiable lives and saving statistical lives."

Public policy inevitably has to accept casualties. We do not ban automobiles, guns, or alcohol despite annual loss of life, because we judge their utility to be greater than their cost. It is seldom an equal weighing. Identified lives loom so much larger because they have a human face. Statistical deaths, no less human and no less dead, do not have a face—only a number. Not nearly as visible, but human nevertheless. It is not good public policy to ignore these "statistics." As one author observed:

> The statistical life is one of the fifty lives that will be lost in a year because of a government decision not to pursue a particular mine safety regulation. The identifiable life is the one miner trapped in the collapsed mine. We are held hostage to these identified lives—much like a kidnapper holds his/her victims hostage. It is hard not to give in to a ransom note. What seems cruel in an individual case is often actually the most lifesaving and compassionate for the general society. (Eddy 1991)

Joseph Stalin once said: "One man's death is a tragedy; a million men's deaths—is a statistic." In a horrible way, Stalin was right, and his reasoning applies to the American health-care system. "We don't mind throwing people overboard," says one wag, "we just don't want to hear the splash." In the same spirit, Governor Kitzhaber has said: "Legislatures have never had to confront the victims of silent rationing or be account-able for the very human consequences. It is like high level bombing where the crew never sees the faces of the people they are killing." (Abramowitz 1992) George Bernard Shaw had it right: we must be educated and compassionate enough to be moved by statistics.

We do many things at great expense to avoid having to say no to identified lives. The United States has approximately three times the percentage of intensive care beds than other industrial nations, and yet we don't save any more of the critically ill. We have far more specialists than other industrial countries. We spend billions of dollars to avoid having to make the everyday life-and-death decisions that other countries make routinely. Then we turn around and leave over 40 million Americans without health insurance.

We spend more billions on expensive neonatology units, often to save preemies who will cost more millions and have little or no quality of life, but we do not give prenatal care to many American women. That is neither good nor compassion-ate health policy.

THE FAILURE OF SUCCESS

Toward the end of his 1998 State of the Union Speech, Presi-dent Bill Clinton issued this challenge in asking for funding for health-care research: "I ask you to support this initiative so ours will be the generation that finally wins the war against cancer, and begins a revolution in our fight against all deadly diseases." A magnificent goal, but it does raise a disturbing question—what are we going to die of, rust? Do we really want to do away with "all deadly diseases?" Is this how we should be spending our resources?

One of the reasons that health care in an aging society is so expensive is that few things in health care have actually saved us money. Marshall McLuhan once observed, "Nothing fails like success." It is worth keeping in mind as we plan for our aging society. A good health-care system actually increases the number of sick people in a society. It decreases mortality, but it increases morbidity. The more successful we are in treating acute disease, the more we must spend treating chronic disease. The faster we run, the farther behind we fall.

Most of our "miracles" of medicine set us up for more expensive health care down the line. Eileen Crimmins makes an important point:

> As mortality declines, those saved from death do not tend to be persons of average constitution but a weaker and frailer group who would have perished under a more severe mortality regime. Thus, with more mortality declines the population becomes more heavily weighted with a frailer group more susceptible to a whole host of diseases and conditions than the average survivor in the population. (Crimmins and Ingegneri 1993)

In other words, good medicine keeps sick and frail people alive, thereby increasing the number and proportion of sick and frail people in the population.

Some studies show that lifetime health-care costs of smokers are less than the lifetime health-care costs of nonsmokers. In any given year, we spend more on health care for smokers because it is a terrible, health-impairing habit. Yet, from a systems standpoint, smokers die efficiently. Smokers, on the average, die eight years before nonsmokers. Smokers generally die of their first or second disease, while the rest of us have four or five serious illnesses before we die a negotiated death in a hospital or nursing home. The same results follow many of our "cures." We have substantially reduced acute disease to throw ourselves into the arms of chronic disease. There is no "cure" for old age. Our medical miracles too often become our fiscal failures.

As Henry J. Aaron and Charles L. Schultz observe:

> Improvements in health habits are highly desirable, but not because they would lower costs. Estimates of the economic consequences of a cessation of smoking, for example, indicate that it would generate small net medical savings at best, and would on balance impose overall social costs. Those spared premature deaths from smoking-induced cancers, heart disease, or other sicknesses would eventually die from other more costly illnesses. Alzheimer's disease, for example, would generate costs even larger on average than those associated with deaths from smoking-induced illnesses. (Aaron and Schultze 2010)

This does not mean we should stop fighting cigarettes. Cigarettes steal health and cause over 400,000 U.S. deaths each year. That is the equivalent to the death toll of eight Vietnams every year. We need a smoke-free America because it will make us more healthy and productive—but it will not, in the long run, save us money. Those 400,000 people still die having consumed far more health care, nursing home care, and Social Security. Dr. Kip Viscusi, a researcher at Duke, found that smokers actually subsidize nonsmokers by dying before collecting their share of retirement and health benefits. We don't want this to be true, but the evidence seems overwhelming. When all costs are taken into account, smoking saves government money.

Similarly, many people mistakenly believe that technology will help us avoid some of these hard choices. This appears to be a mistaken hope. Technology enhances the things we can do to aging bodies, but it seldom saves us money. As one scholar observes:

> In most industries, technological innovations are welcomed without question because they generally lead to a less expensive or more efficient production process....

> However, most technological innovations in the health service industry have added to rather than reduced costs ... the question is not whether recent technological developments have added to health care costs—they have. The real question is whether the benefits exceed the costs, and in at least some instances they may not. (Riddick and Cordes 1980)

Neonatology miraculously saves 500-gram babies, but it also gives us yearly a significant new number of disabled people. We save people from heart attacks at 75 to have them die of Alzheimer's disease at 85. Because we all must die of something, almost every "success" ends up costing us more health care dollars (and usually more Social Security dollars).

There will always be ten leading causes of death. Sulfa drugs caused a steep decline in the death rate from pneumonia, but preventing fatalities from pneumonia has had the effect of increasing the average duration and expense of other illnesses: senile brain disease, arteriosclerosis, hypertension, diabetes, and similar diseases of aging. So, also with preventive care: Cost effectiveness studies, which estimate the net costs and net health benefits of interventions, show that preventive care usually increases medical expenditures.

The Population Reference Bureau published a 1984 study, "Death and Taxes," which found that curing cancer and curing heart disease would increase federal spending. The authors were not arguing that we should not try, but they wanted us to do it fully realizing the consequences. They found that "the postponement of death increases federal costs, requiring more taxes." Like Faust, we were not fully aware of the tradeoffs.

Yes, we should continue to "cure" disease, but we cannot "cure" death. Chronic disease at the end of life is far more expensive than acute disease in mid-life. An aging society needs a deeper dialogue on how we set limits. Not setting some limits on "high cost/low benefit" procedure will surely waste limited funds and negatively affect our children.

An aging, inventive society, which is already borrowing heavily from our children to fund government, and whose economy faces massive international competition, must start a dialogue on how it allocates its scarce financial resources. A society that in the last thirty years has doubled the health-care share of its GNP must start to realistically look at its options for stabilizing those growth trends. We do not have the luxury of merely tinkering at the margins.

I absolutely believe that in this age of technological miracles, no health-care system can give every citizen all the existing beneficial health care. We must find ways to set limits or our entire economy will become even more unbalanced toward health care. In 1960, the United States spent 6 percent of its GDP on health care; in 2018, it climbed to 19 percent of GDP. Government has many obligations to perform in a modern society (education, the justice system, infrastructure, etc.), and it already spends a disproportionate amount on health care. Limits must be set!

Yet, I wake up every morning next to the most important person in my life who was saved from breast cancer by modern medicine. In addition, my grandson Kennon was born with hydrocephaly and was saved by a shunt in his brain. He is now an energetic and talented eleven-year-old thanks to modern medicine.

So I rejoice at what medicine has done for my family yet recognize that is has the potential to crowd out many other necessary services of government, possibly bankrupting our government entirely.

This subject has consumed much of my time and energy since the mid-1980s.

CAMBODIAN REFUGEE RELIEF

Dottie and I spent some time in Cambodia on our trip around the world in 1967. Then, in early 1979, when the "killing fields" were in the news, Dottie and I were in China on a goodwill trip, and when that was over we went to Thailand and up the border of Cambodia, accompanied by the US Ambassador to Thailand in his helicopter. As I was a governor, he extended every courtesy.

We admired the kind, polite, and generous people of Cambodia; we were in awe of their archaeology, and were immensely impressed by Ankor Wat. And we had followed from afar the disruption of Cambodia caused in part by US bombing.

At the border, we saw sights that haunted us for years. Piles of dead bodies, starving people pouring across the border. Although the refugee relief workers were taking good care of the people who made it across the border, they were well aware of how many people were dying along the way. We met one old, emaciated old woman who had fled the killings fields with her teenage grandson—her only surviving relative. Weeks into their journey, with just enough food to keep them from complete starvation, they arrived at the border across from the tent colony we were visiting. They were literally at the end of their endurance and the end of their journey when her grandson stepped on a land mine and was killed. Beyond horror.

We returned to the United States and started to do a considerable amount of fund-raising for Cambodian relief. I developed a slide show from photos I took while there and showed it widely around Colorado. Denver businessman Phil Anschutz alone gave $35,000. I hated raising money for myself and for politics, but for this cause, it was a labor of love. I gave it as much time and energy as I could consistent with my duties as governor. About ten years later, both Dottie and I were named "Humanist of the Year" for two years running by the American Humanist Society for our work.

But as the realities of global warming began to emerge, I developed a new viewpoint on refugees. It rises not from a hard heart but from the full realization of what global warming is going to do to the life-support systems of our planet.

Another issue that transcends my role as a politician is the stark reality of global warming and how to reconcile that with the future of the human race. The following piece, originally published in the *Denver Post* in 2017, lays out my thinking.

THE BRAVE NEW WORLD OF SUSTAINABILITY ETHICS

Let me be blunt: human rights as they have developed over the last seventy years cannot survive global warming. This is an apocalyptic vision but an important viewpoint that needs new debate. The triumph of human rights has been one of the great ethical victories of the last century. They have saved countless lives and helped stay the hand of many vicious dictators. It has truly made the world more "human." Tragically but realistically, we must debate anew their applicability in a crowded, warming world.

Climate change, poverty, civil war and civil strife, drought, and myriad other threats are causing massive movement of people. The Mediterranean crisis these past two summers are likely a preview of the dislocation to come. It is not too apocalyptic to consider the possibility that ultimately a warming world may not be able to support 7 billion people (current) or 9.5 billion (projected) by 2050. The problems caused by climate change are likely to be of unprecedented magnitude. The Pentagon issued a report as far back as 2002 that stated, "Abrupt climate change is likely to stretch (the earth's) carrying capacity well beyond its already precarious limits." In this new reality, how many dislocated people can any nation take without ruining its own economic and social fabric? How do we even think about such a dilemma?

The classic metaphor of human caring is the "Good Samaritan" where a beaten and injured traveler is helped by a Samaritan after the victim is ignored by two other religious men. The good Samaritan binds his wounds and pays out of his own pocket for the man's shelter and recovery. There are few, if any, more frequently cited ethical examples.

But what if instead of one injured traveler, there were twenty or fifty? How do we even think about such a dilemma? What if this is the metaphor for the world we will soon face? The world does a totally inadequate job caring for the sixty million refugees it has now. Europe's politics have already been seriously impacted. Compassion fatigue has already set in and the warming only promises to get worst.

The environmental and human rights community over-whelmingly recognizes the reality of global warming, but few venture to address its almost inevitable consequences on refu-gee policy. What happens when hundreds of millions of people are dislocated by flooding, starvation, and chaos? The melting of the glaciers in the Himalayas threatens the food supply of as many as two billion people. There are no lessons from the past that can guide us in the new world of dislocation we are approaching. We are sailing into uncharted ethical waters.

Is it not hubris to think that humans are the only species that can grow without limits? The population of sub-Saharan Africa is expected to double in the next thirty years. Similarly, high birth rates and political unrest in most of the Middle East and Africa suggest continued massive migration from those volatile areas. Is Europe's only ethical response to take them all in? Same question for the United States. Is the Statue of Liberty an endless invitation to all? Forever?

One of the great challenges of history is to know when a new paradigm has emerged. I believe we face such a paradigm shift as we move from infinite growth to human sustainability. Public policy cannot, ultimately, be at variance with ecological reality and this will require a whole rethinking of our eco-nomic, social, and ethical assumptions. Our public policy must, at some undefined point, adapt to our ecological system, or at a minimum our economic system cannot destroy our ecological system. We are at the threshold of such a new world.

Perhaps with our oceans warming, deserts creeping, and our seas rising, it is time to debate if and how our ethical principles fit into a finite world challenged by infinite demand. Would not this new world of limits require us to rethink the very basis of our current ethics and public policy? What would this mean to our cherished concepts of individual and human rights? How would the emergence of ecological limits alter our long-held ethical beliefs? Would that not mean that ultimately nature, not reason, becomes the framework for both? But nature has no "ethics."

Our standard of living, our economic system, our political stability require expanding use of energy and resources, and much of our political, economic, and social thinking assumes infinite expansion of population and economic activity with little or no restraint on resource use. We all feel entitled to grow richer every year. Our concept of social justice requires an expanded pie to share with the less fortunate. Progress is growth and the economy of all developed nations requires steady increases in consumption. What if this scenario is unsustainable and the new reality forces the world to learn to live with finitude?

I am impressed by a scholar named Herschel Eliott who explored the world beyond all "human centered ethics." Human hubris notwithstanding, Elliott suggests we ultimately must live within a limited and increasingly fragile ecosystem. He sees chaos ahead, saying, "We are unlikely to be the first species in the world to be exempt from ecological limits." Elliott doubts that growth can ultimately solve growth-related problems and that we must move to sustainability in both our public policy and our thinking. Elliott believes that if this ever happens, it will require us to reject much of the paradigm on which the human-centered ethical thinking of Western culture is based.

Elliott believes that our moral thinking historically has been set in the domain of abstract thought and reasoned judgment. Traditional ethics assume a world without limits and are based on reason. But in a world of limits, public policy must not only make moral sense but ecological sense. No morality can demand what the ecosystem cannot support. We cannot ignore the real-world consequences of our abstract beliefs, argues Elliott. We cannot have a moral duty to supply something where by the act of supplying it, we further harm the ecosystem and make life on earth unsustainable. We cannot disregard the factual consequences of what we have come to think of as "moral" behavior. If acting "moral" causes further compromise to the ecosystem, that "moral" behavior must be rethought because ethics cannot demand resource use that the ecosystem cannot support.

Elliott believes that "a priori, human centered ethics" are unsustainable in a finite ecosystem and that at some point nature's laws will trump human ethics. Nature does truly bat last. He postulates that no ethical system or value system can be valid if it cumulatively destroys the ecosystem of which it is a part. As Elliott points out: "The culture of growth that drives the ethical, political, economic thinking in the Western nations confuses the two domains (mental world and physical world). It assumes the open-ended, infinite expansion that is possible in the mental-cultural domain is also possible in the physical world." (Elliott and Lamm 2002)

This is a new world and regardless how laudatory and well-meaning current human rights doctrine is, the ecosystem will not give priority to humans over every other living thing. That is not nature's way of operating. But will not human ingenuity and imagination solve these problems? "It is extremely improbable that human ingenuity could devise a system that would be as stable and secure as the one which nature has already designed. The new human system would be unlikely to function for more than a few ticks of geological time." (Elliott and Lamm 2002)

Elliott believes that neither religious nor ethical thinking can trump ecological limits. "When the man-made bio-system fails because of some ethical misconception about how human beings ought to live in the world, it will be irrelevant that Christians, Muslims and Jews had believed that the true morality was revealed to man in the eternal word of God. It will be beside the point that professionals in ethics and philosophy had used the demands of conscience and the self-evident truths of reason … to justify their moral convictions about how human beings ought to live and act." (Elliott and Lamm 2002)

Elliott is right. We cannot avoid the collective consequences of wrong assumptions. Humans are likely on a march
to a tragic destination. Neither population growth nor economic growth can go on indefinitely. The ecosystem has little
use for our elegantly reasoned ethical systems. To be valid,
public policy and ethics must be sustainable. "The fact is that
if the practice of a mistaken conception of ethics should ever
allow the world's life-
support system to break
down, nature's experiment
with homo sapiens would
be over. If living by a
system of ethics should
make human life physically
impossible, that ethics is
absurd." (Elliott and Lamm
2002)

STATE OF THE STATE SPEECH
AT THE CAPITOL, 1980

We must reconcile our
thinking and culture to the
ecological system that sur-
rounds us. No matter how
attractive and elegantly
reasoned is the world of
our historic vision, it ultimately
must fit within the reality of the
physical world. This would be a new world where much of our
economy and our social systems would have to be rethought.

Our ethics (and concepts of right and wrong) have been
formulated in a thought world, the world of Kant and "a priori"
reasoning. Reason alone dictates our ethics and disregards all
physical constraints. But that doesn't mean that they are not
there. You may passionately believe that there are no limits and
that population growth and economic growth can go on forever, but you must also consider: What if you are wrong? Ethical behavior has to be not only rational but also ecological.
We are living on the shoulders of some awesome exponential
curves. No ethical code can demand of humans duties and

behaviors that nature cannot support. We need to construct a moral code based not on human rights but on human sustainability. It will be a Copernican undertaking.

We should start this exploration now. Moral codes, no matter how logical and reasoned, and human rights, no matter how compassionate, must live and make sense within the limitations of the ecosystem. Moral life cannot be constructed solely in a thought world: it has to also make ecological sense. But to set forth that the old rules of human rights and Kantian analysis has to be rethought doesn't mean that no rules apply. It should not mean a return to the laws of the jungle. Geopolitics require that we help deal with problems that, at least in the case of global warming, we helped cause. Few argue with the principle that a nation owes its first duty to its own citizens, but we also can't be an island of plenty amidst a world of chaos. We have done very little thinking about what happens if global warming or peak oil manifest themselves in societal breakdown.

The West needs a dose of reality therapy. The maximum generosity of the developed world can't begin to meet the refugee demand of a warming world. This year, perhaps, but the problem promises to stretch for decades. It is a Sisyphean problem and needs an honest dialogue. Is Europe doomed to absorb all or part of the high birth rates south of its borders? Why? How many people dislocated by global warming does even a compassionate America take? Yes, we helped cause a warming world, but does that mean we must commit demographic suicide?

Whatever the answer, it is time for a new debate on refugee policy in a warming world. These issues will not go away; they will only grow worse. Likely on a steep time line. It cannot be thought of in usual terms. The dilemma of public policy is most of our problems weigh heavily on our future, but all our experience lies in the past. Humanity never gets to rest on its oars, new problems always arise but never at the pace and velocity that we face now. It will be like changing a tire while the car is still moving.

IMMIGRATION: THE ULTIMATE
ENVIRONMENTAL ISSUE

Every generation has its challenges, almost inevitably challenges different from those of its parent's generation. The great
challenge of public policy is to correctly identify the new challenges and the new realities that society is faced with. Public
policy is a kaleidoscope, and time changes the patterns we are
faced with and we have to be wise enough to react to the new
challenges as these new patterns evolve.

As I discuss in my *Denver Post* article (above), one new
pattern/challenge must be to look at the issue of the environment with new eyes. [Our globe is under dramatic new environmental pressure: our globe is warming, our ice caps melting,
our glaciers receding, our coral is dying, our soils are eroding,
our water tables falling, our fisheries are being depleted, our
remaining rain forests shrinking. Something is very, very wrong
with our ecosystem. The environment issue is hydra-headed
and complicated, but it is of immense importance that we have
all aspects of the issue on the table. Margaret Thatcher, who
read chemistry at Oxford, was one new and important Conservative voice calling for new thinking. In her speech to the 2nd
World Climate Conference in 1990, she stated:

> The threat to our world comes not only from tyrants and
> their tanks, it can be more insidious though less visible.
> The danger of global warming is as yet unseen, but real
> enough for us to make changes and sacrifices so that we
> do not live at the expense of future generations.
>
> Our ability to come together to stop or limit damage
> to the world's environment will be perhaps the greatest
> test of how far we can act as a world community. No-
> one should under-estimate the imagination that will be
> required, nor the scientific effort, nor the unprecedent-
> ed co-operation we shall have to show.

One issue in the current environmental debate, however, is strangely absent: immigration. Immigration is the ultimate environmental issue, but the environmental leaders are AWOL on this issue. The United States with low immigration will stabilize its population at about 360 million by the middle of this century. With current levels of immigration it will double and then double again. The Census projections call

for an America of 420 million people by 2050 and a billion by the end of this century. Can you imagine the ecosystem, already under great strain, with 1 billion consuming Americans? We are leaving our grandchildren an unsustainable America of a billion people, which I suggest is public policy malpractice.

The environmental community wouldn't tell you this (though most know). A combination of political correctness and the recent tendency of the environmental leadership to play Democratic poli-

ON THE CAMPAIGN TRAIL, 1978

tics have silenced the almost universal recognition of the early environmental community that population was an indispensable part of environmentalism.

Environmental leaders in the 1960s had a formula, I=PAT, which postulated that environmental impact was the sum of POPULATION, AFFLUENCE, and TECHNOLOGY. To former US Senator Gaylord Nelson (D Wisconsin), who conceived Earth Day, and the early environmental leaders, leaving out population would be like having a bicycle with only one wheel. Today's environmentalists will discuss US air pollution policy, US wilderness policy, US water quality policy, US billboard policy, but never a hint of US population policy.

Here's my simple experiment I use on my environmental friends who have tragically lost their voice on population. Assume that I had a magic wand and could wave it and accomplish all the goals of today's environmental leadership, but did nothing about the current immigration rate. Is there a scenario where a billion Americans at the end of this century would live in an environmentally sound America? Have you been to China? India? We could do everything they suggest yet still have an unlivable nation.

There is a concerted effort in the environmental community to keep immigration out of the dialogue. But the subject is so central to the environment that it keeps popping out. The President's Council on Sustainable Development concluded in 1996 that "we believe that reducing current immigration levels is a necessary part of working toward sustainability in the United States." National commissions have made similar assessments since 1972.

The National Academy of Sciences and the Royal Society have also warned that increasing population and increasing consumption threaten to overshoot the earth's ecological carrying capacity. In my view most of the historic ways that societies have grown and developed may be obsolete, and if they are, we are overdriving our headlights and heading for major traumas. Shouldn't we at least discuss it?

Why do we want to double the size of America and then double it again? Imagine for a minute that we had taken the advice of President Nixon's Commission on Population Growth (the Rockefeller Commission) and the American Future released in 1972. The commission recommended, among other things, that America act to end illegal immigration and to freeze legal immigration at 400,000 a year. The commission found that "the health of our country does not depend on population growth, nor does the vitality of business, nor the welfare of the average person." Strong words. Wise words.

Headed by John Rockefeller, the "Rockefeller Commission" as it was known, strongly urged stabilizing the population of the United States and asked Americans to get over their "ideological addiction to growth." America at that time had about 200 million Americans, used far less petroleum, and had a much smaller "ecological footprint" on the world environment. But the nation didn't listen to the commission.

It is unfortunate that American policy makers didn't listen. We have added approximately 100 million Americans since the commission's brave and farsighted declaration. What problem in contemporary America was made better by population growth and immigration asks C.U. Physics Professor Al Bartlett? We now have almost 330 million Americans, we consume far more non-renewable resources, and our "ecological footprint" is one of the major factors in a deteriorating environment worldwide.

The geometry is relentless. The first census (in 1790) found 4 million Europeans in America. Two hundred years (1990) later we had approximately 260 million Americans. That means we had six doublings of the original European population. Please note that two more doublings give us over a billion people sharing America.

There are a number of people who postulate that our current population of 300 million Americans is not itself sustainable, let alone 420 million or a billion. Sustainability looks at the long term: will our resources allow 300 million Americans to live a satisfying life at a decent level of living for the indefinite future? Will our children and grandchildren inherit a decent and livable America? We have not only put this question off limits, we have made it taboo.

This is not an issue of immigrants, but of immigration. What possible public policy advantage would there be to an America of 500 million? Do we lack for people? Do we have too much open space? Too much parkland and recreation? What will 500 million Americans mean to our environment? There are similar nonenvironmental questions. Do we need a larger military? Are our schools unpopulated? Do we not have enough diversity? Will we live better lives if your city doubles in size? Does immigration help our health-care system? Do you want an America of one billion people? These questions seem to answer themselves.

I do not believe you can have infinite population growth in a finite world. We are living on the shoulders of some awesome geometric curves. The 2000 census revealed how rapidly immigration is causing our population to skyrocket. The equivalent of another California has been added to the nation—32 million people since 1990. Demographers calculate that immigration is now the determining factor in causing America's rapid population growth—immigrants and their U.S. born children accounted for more than two-thirds of population growth in the last decade, and will continue to account for approximately two-thirds of our future growth. Clearly, America's population "growth issue" is an immigration issue.

The environmental problems just around the corner will require new, bold, creative leadership. There was a zoo in the 1960s, which put up a sign in part of the exit complex, which said "See the World's Most Dangerous Animal," and you went around the corner and there was a full-length mirror. Humans are the world's most dangerous animals. Similarly, I am haunted by a casual remark that the great biologist E. O. Wilson made. Wilson observed that the human species is the only species that, were it to disappear, every other species would benefit. I suspect this is true. The human species has itself become the chief change agent of the environment. As Margaret Thatcher implied: we face an environmental world where all past is prologue.

Will we be able to adapt in time? History shows that humans have successfully faced many challenges. I believe that many of the great and wise sayings concerning the importance of history, like Santayana's statement that "those who cannot remember the past are condemned to repeat it," or Harry Truman's quote to the effect that the only surprises in the future are the history you don't know—while perhaps still true for human events, do not give us guidance on our major environmental public policy challenges and can be downright dangerous as we face the next generation of public issues. In some ways history has become a trap because it prevents us from recognizing the full seriousness of the problems we are faced with. An old world is dying and a new world in which history is of limited use, is struggling to be born. Heretical words but let me make my case.

History does teach us much about human nature, about humanities, ambitions, cruelties, follies, about the seduction of power, the temptation of riches and lust. We enlarge our knowledge and enrich our soul by the study of history. History has been an important part of my life.

But history does not teach us about Mother Nature; it does not allow us to properly evaluate something like global warming, environmental degradation, or the growth of human numbers. A study of history would not have predicted the Renaissance, or the Industrial Revolution when they burst upon humankind, and I don't believe it is of much help in the search for the new world of sustainability.

The past gives little guidance to the next generation of environmental problems because we are living on the upper shoulder of some unprecedented and dangerous geometric curves. We ignore Professor Al Bartlett's wise words that the greatest human failure is our inability to understand the exponential function. I believe the next sequences of geometric growth in human numbers and environmental impact are unsustainable, and are thus by definition without precedent. The relentless cascade of geometry is giving us a world beyond historical precedent. History teaches us of human limitations, but not of nature's limits. History gives us little guide to a world that needs to turn from "growth" to "sustainability." Some guidance, of course, but not where it really counts. We are sailing on uncharted waters.

I believe that we are surrounded with evidence that increasingly shows that something is fundamentally wrong with our historic ways of looking at the world. Yesterday's solutions have become today's problems, and these problems are of a different scale and coming at us with increasing velocity. The growth paradigm that allowed us to create wealth, reduce poverty, and increase living standards is becoming obsolete. Those human traits that allowed us to prevail over the ice, the tiger and the bear—in a time of an empty earth continue to operate long after we are no longer an empty earth.

Reg Morrison in his book, *The Spirit of the Gene*, suggests that those genes that saved a species now are on course to destroy us. He suggests that we are hardwired by survival traits to grow and overconsume and that now, unless controlled, these traits will drive us into oblivion. Evolution moves too slowly to correct the dilemma that evolution put us in by its past slow progress.

When I entered high school in 1950, there were 2.6 billion people on earth, and there were 50 million cars. Now there are over 7 billion people on earth, and our car population has increased tenfold to 500 million; and within 25 years it is projected there will be 1 billion cars on the world's roads. (Youngquist 1997)

Nothing in our past prepares us for the environmental problems that we are faced with. We cannot grow our way out of these problems; we cannot use history to put them into perspective. The lessons we have learned living on an empty earth teach us the wrong lessons. We are still trying to "be fruitful, multiply, and subdue" an earth that now needs saving. Contemporary life is a rock rolling downhill, gathering speed. It presents us with a series of problems of nature, for which the lessons of history are not only useless, but teach us the wrong lessons.

The famous economist Kenneth Boulding said that the modern human dilemma is that all our experience deals with the past, yet all our problems are challenges of the future. The lessons we have learned in the past do not help and in many ways are counterproductive in solving the problems of sustainability. Our economic models have become ecologically unsustainable.

Humans appear throughout history to be insatiable creatures. There appears at this time to be no reasonable limit on "more," "bigger," or "faster" or "richer." If we haven't already hit carrying capacity, it is just a matter of time.

We cannot solve growth-related problems with more growth; we must move to sustainability. It took a billion years or more for nature to create the limited stocks of petroleum and mineral wealth which modern technology and human ingenuity have recently learned to exploit. But we are squandering our one time inheritance of cheap energy and handy resources. The models so painstakingly developed over 300 years to create more jobs and more goods and services must be dramatically modified.

"In every age," writes Bronowski (1973), in *The Ascent of Man*, "there is a turning point, a new way of seeing and asserting the coherence of the world." We metaphorically must give birth to a whole new world. Our new environmental issues, like global warming, will not just take a legislative victory or public awareness campaign, it will take a revolution in the way we see and make sense of our basic civilization and the human role in the universe.

What to do? At a minimum we should move to stabilize the population of the United States and the planet. I can't believe that the Trump administration is going around the world discouraging condom use and teaching "natural family planning."

I believe that we should have a $2 per gallon tax on gasoline, the proceeds of which would not be available for new governmental spending but instead to help us retire the baby boomers, which is another great challenge facing America.

I believe we should abolish most of the income tax, except on the higher incomes, and move more to consumption taxes. We must reuse, recycle, restore. We shouldn't build a car in America that doesn't get forty miles per gallon. Alternative energy sources are available and easily developed with the right public policy. Energy guru Amory Lovins says that alternative energy is not only a free lunch, but also one that we get paid to eat. We must reduce immigration from the current levels of mass immigration (1.3 million a year) to numbers closer to our historical averages (270,000 a year). We must stress community, and use religion and spirituality to become less materialistic. Is this enough? No, of course not, but you get the idea. It is not exactly a politically popular agenda, but a necessary one.

But first of all, we must better practice humility, appreciate better what we don't know (ignorance), and develop a culture of limits. We in the West can help give birth to the new world that will be required on the downslide of the Hubbert curve. The West has had its own clash of cultures that track the knowledge/ignorance dilemma: the culture of the infinite and living with the finite.

Civilization has triumphed in the West because it has refused to accept limits and has overcome a myriad of obstacles. Our ancestors found a desert and made it into a garden. The culture of the infinite teaches that knowledge, ingenuity, and imagination can prevail over any obstacles and that there are no limits—only lack of creativity.

This is the West of irrigation canals, trans mountain diversions, pivot sprinklers, and other adaptations that allow us not only to live in a semidesert but also to enjoy green lawns and prosperity. The culture of the infinite suggests the future is a logical extension of the past, that all problems have achievable solutions: "Go forth and multiply and subdue the earth" and "Go West, young man."

It is the optimism of, "Not to worry: God gave man two hands and only one stomach." It reflects a devout belief in limitless economic development, progress, and the perfectibility of the human condition. It is the world of the green revolution that has given us the potential to eliminate hunger, and of technology that some say has repealed the law of supply and demand and discovered endless and unlimited wealth. This is the world built around unlimited people—unsatisfied consumers.

The supporters of the infinite are either the modern prophets or the modern alchemists—but to date they say they have been stunningly successful in solving the problem of population and poverty. And in their minds their approach will continue to be successful. Knowledge trumps all! Aridity can be solved by desalinating oceans, and wealth (computer chips) can be created out of sand.

The second culture is the culture of the finite. The West also teaches that we must adapt to nature and be acutely aware of nature's fickleness and limitations. It teaches us humility and caution, that there is such a thing as "carrying capacity," and we must respect the fragility of the land and environment. It argues that nature teaches us that we never can or should rely on knowledge or the status quo, that climate is harsh and variable, and that the price of survival is to humbly recognize, anticipate, and to the extent possible, prepare for the surprises that nature has in store for us. It questions the proposition that growth, population or economic, can go on forever. This is the world of conservation, national parks, wilderness legislation, crop rotation, Planned Parenthood, Malthus, and the *Exxon Valdez*. It is the vision of Thomas Berry: "The earth and the human community are bound in a single journey." And it listens to Isaiah: "Woe unto them that lay field upon field and house upon house that there be no place to be left alone in the world."

Our industrial civilization is built upon the assumptions that there are no limits, that technology will forever solve our problems, and that we will not reach any sort of carrying capacity. It assumes infinite resources, where scarcity is caused by want of knowledge and imagination. Civilization in most of the world supports this assumption of the infinite.

The finite culture, with fewer adherents, but equally passionate, contends that the first culture is making "empty earth" assumptions that cannot be sustained. They point out that the more we know, the more we don't know, and that technological hubris is dangerous to our future. They want to move now to stabilize US population, reduce our energy use, and help the rest of the world do likewise.

Ultimately, finite-culture adherents feel that we cannot and should not have an America of 500 million living our consumptive lifestyles. They contend that we live in a hinge of history where society must rewrite the entire script. If they are correct, then our basic assumptions about life, our great religious traditions, and our economy are conceptually obsolete. So far, those who sing this song are failed prophets.

But what if—just what if—the culture of the infinite was only a temporary victor? What if nature bats last? What if the real lesson we should have learned in a place with thirteen inches of rain was the need to appreciate that limits could be pushed and extended but never eliminated? What if the rain forests, the dying coral, the rising temperatures are trying to tell us something?

The lessons I have learned from my love affair with the West support this second culture. I believe we need to transform society from an earth-consuming technological civilization to a sustainable and more benign civilization. I'm impressed with Aldo Leopold's "land ethic," which teaches that human fate depends on our ability to change the basic values, beliefs, and aspirations of the total society. I believe that the fate of the world depends on our ability to know when to abandon the infinite culture, and shift to the finite culture. Wait too long and we are doomed. Some will say if we shift too soon, we'll give up a lot of fun and exhilaration. I'd rather we shift too soon. We won't get a chance to shift too late. Let me end by quoting Howard Nemerov, a former Poet Laureate:

> Praise without end for the go-ahead zeal of whoever it was invented the wheel; but never a word for the poor soul's sake that thought ahead and invented the brake.

5. BACK IN THE FRAY: POLITICAL BACKLASH

FISCAL HARDWIRING

I was born in Madison, Wisconsin, in 1935, where my father worked for the Franchise Tax Board as a certified public accountant (CPA) assigned to audit large companies for the state of Wisconsin. Looking back at my youth, I recognize two influences that help explain my political career and my thinking on issues. The first is that my father, who was raised in poverty, had lost all his money at the beginning of the Depression. My parents were newly married and were struggling but saving when the "bank holiday" hit. They lost everything, but my father still had a job, so the trauma to our family was minor compared to the majority of Americans. He just kept on working and started saving all over again. But the loss of all his assets definitely affected his thinking about borrowing and investing, and that conservatism was handed down to me and my brothers. I hated borrowing money and paid all mortgages and loans off as quickly as possible. We would have been much better off if we had learned to use borrowed money as an investment tool, but I just couldn't feel comfortable doing so. I have bought three Denver houses and two mountain homes in my life, and I paid down the mortgages on all of them as soon as possible. Perhaps a mistake, but it also impacted the way I looked at governmental debt.

I should have been self-aware enough not to have ever entered the 1992 US Senate race. But, Tim Wirth, after one spectacular term in the Senate, had shocked our political world by announcing that he would not run for reelection. He wrote a very poignant piece in the *New York Times* about how he disliked the political part of the job and how much of his time was consumed by fund-raising. Meanwhile, there was pressure from a lot of people and organizations for me to run. So I did. It was the only campaign in which I felt uncomfortable all the time.

Meaning to go back to the private life I had so much enjoyed, I had not run for a fourth term as governor. I like neither the pace nor the style of modern politics. Twelve years was enough! I loved my academic life and dreaded the campaign. Why did I say yes? It is hard to reconstruct, but I had not fully recognized how much I had come to hate campaigning and fund-raising.

The situation was complicated by Congressman Ben Nighthorse Campbell getting into the race, soon to be followed by Josie Heath, a woman I had known from college days and who felt strongly that the Senate needed more women. I literally hated the campaign: constant fund-raising, arguments among friends, and endless hours of campaigning. I of course knew this from the beginning and rate this as one of the great misjudgments of my life. Congressman Campbell won the primary and went on to be elected to the US Senate. I was secretly relieved and was soon back into my private life.

POPULATION AND IMMIGRATION

I believe I would have won the 1992 Senate race had it not been for my consuming interest in population and immigration. (See Chapter 4 for more on my views on these issues; e.g., my 2017 article from the *Denver Post*.) It ultimately tipped the scales against me, and that is the way democracy is supposed to work. But even now, I have trouble convincing friends that immigration is an important issue. Especially now that President Trump has turned this issue into a xenophobic tirade.

I had previously had great success in anticipating important issues. Abortion, health care, physician aid in dying, the environment, and political reform are all issues that I was an early advocate of, and not only had I survived them, I had thrived. But I recognized the danger of being ahead of one's time in a democracy. I used to say, "A politician can't be so far ahead of the band that they can't hear the music!" It finally caught up with me. I got too far ahead of the band.

Shortly after being elected governor, I had a memorable meeting with a large group of Hispanic Coloradans who had just been fired from a local meat-packing plant. The plant then went on to replace these Americans with illegal aliens. As I remember, the Americans were getting paid eight dollars per hour plus some minimal benefits, whereas the illegal workers were getting paid five dollars an hour, with no benefits. This offended my sense of justice. Illegal immigration was undercutting American workers and creating downward pressure on their wages. My Labor Department added insult to injury when they informed me that a large percentage of illegal workers were paid in cash and escaped our withholding taxes. Yet they created demand for services and most had kids in our school system. Most Coloradans fail to recognize how much it costs to allow these individuals to break the law. Every child in our school system costs the regular per capita costs plus the costs of hiring Spanish-speaking teachers and staff. Illegal immigration is about cheap labor, and these employers slough off the costs of public services on the public. Ever since that moment I have opposed illegal immigration.

But I also sought to reduce legal immigration. It seemed so clear to me that most Americans don't want to double the size of America's population. Two national commissions (appointed by President Reagan and President Clinton, as well as Congress) had reached the near-unanimous conclusion that America should not tolerate illegal immigration ("we are a nation of laws"), and that legal immigration should be reduced to more absorbable numbers. Both commissions, one headed by Father Theodore Hesburgh, president of Notre Dame University, and one by Congresswoman Barbara Jordan of Texas, both well-respected liberals, recommended that legal immigration be cut approximately in half, that we should end "chain immigration," and that we should put a new emphasis on the skills of immigrants. Common sense, I thought. Who could argue with these findings?

But I was wrong. I had failed to fully appreciate how deeply ingrained the Statute of Liberty had become in the mind of the general public. "Do you really want to double the population of America and then double it again?" I would ask. "Oh, no, but we have the Statute of Liberty!" they would reply. "Yes," I would respond, "but it was given to America to symbolize liberty, not immigration! It is a tradition, but we are no longer an empty continent with free land. We have largely filled up America, and now the circumstances are so very different. We no longer need people to fill up this once vast and sparsely populated land!" On and on I would argue, often getting nowhere. How many immigrants do we have to take to satisfy the Statute of Liberty? Some people argue whoever wants to come: it is an open-ended promise to the world. Insanity!

FINDING AUDACITY

One of the biggest traumas of my high school years was that I didn't make the football team. In retrospect, it seems silly, but it was a big deal at the time. There went my social status and my dating life in one fell swoop. What self-respecting girl would even look at a failed football player? Something major would have to be done, so I worked that summer in a fishing camp far out in the Ontario wilderness whose only access was by floatplane. A great adventure for a sixteen-year-old.

Back home, this failed football player would find just the right way to drop into conversation how lonely I had been under a full moon on the Great Lakes or how I saw E. E. Cummings across a bar in Greenwich Village, and slowly my social life and self-respect picked up. I really did have some exciting adventures, and most of my football-playing friends had never lived beyond Pittsburgh.

But the most important piece of my early story was that I became a risk-taker. I would hitchhike to most of these places, find a place to live, and find a job—all in a strange town. Otto von Bismarck once said that "success was the child of audacity," and I became audacious. I learned to stretch myself and to welcome a challenge. And I am convinced much of my career happened partly because I was cut from the football squad.

I think back at the many times it was heart-aching lonely becoming a man. On the ore boats on the Great Lakes, under a full moon in Venice after leaving my college girlfriend Ingrid in Norway, in Berkeley watching San Francisco under a full moon and spending Christmas alone in my 1st year of law school in San Francisco. Then, before the soul has had time to adjust, to be constantly surrounded by people wanting a piece of my day. Emotional whiplash then, but eventually worked out to a wonderful balance. I now recognize that my default position is to be alone and/or alone with Dottie.

BACKLASH

Not only had I underestimated the power of the immigration issue, I was totally unprepared for how many people would accuse me of xenophobia and racism. Many of these were my liberal friends, and they knew better. We had been in the civil rights movement together. However, the emotional nature of this issue sweeps in a large array of people, and it is always easy to scramble an issue. The Southern Poverty Law Center is an expert on immigration slander, and regardless of how often the press has called them out on this, they accuse anyone interested in immigration reform as a "racist." I often wonder how many immigrants you had to be in favor of welcoming to avoid their tar brush. Barbara Jordan a racist? Father Hesburgh? My interest has always been demographic, and has become increasingly so as global warming has gone from conjecture to fact. I can find no public policy reasons why we would want to double the size of America's population. I worry now, in a time of automation, computers, and artificial intelligence, where we are going to get the jobs for our children and grandchildren. Yes, immigration has a mixed history, and the laws passed in the 1920s give off more than the scent of racism. But issues change as circumstances change. I believe it is insanity to continue adding people in a time of global warming and technological revolution. Call me wrong, but give me the respect for the thrust of my argument. I believe we should try our best to stop illegal immigration, to cut legal immigration in half, and to choose our immigrants for their skills rather than who they are related to. History, I stand pat!

CONFRONTING FINITUDE

Today, our standard of living, our economic system, and the political stability of our planet all require the increasing use of energy and natural resources. In addition, much of our political, economic, and social thinking assumes a continuous expansion of economic activity with little or no restraint on our use of resources. We all feel entitled to grow richer every year. Social justice requires an expanding pie to share with those who are less fortunate. Progress is growth; the economy of all developed nations requires steady increases in consumption.

What if such a scenario is unsustainable? What if we need an ethics for a finite world? Bottom line, what if the 1992 "Scientists' Warning to Humanity" was correct and "that a great change in our stewardship of the earth and the life on it is required if vast human misery is to be avoided"? (Union of Concerned Scientists 1997)

You may believe that current rates of population growth and economic expansion can go on forever, but debate with me what alternative ethical theories would arise if they cannot. My thesis is that any ethical system is mistaken and immoral if its practice should cause an environmental collapse.

Many people assume that moral laws and principles are absolutely certain, that we know the final moral truth. If moral knowledge is certain, then factual evidence is irrelevant, for it cannot limit or refute what is morally certain. But I agree with Derek Parfit, who in *Reasons and Persons* (1984) said, "Some people believe that there cannot be progress in Ethics, since everything has already been said. I believe the opposite. Compared with the other sciences, Non-Religious Ethics is the youngest and least advanced."

SPEAKING AT A CHARITY DINNER

Our ethics and concepts of human rights have been formulated for a world of a priori reasoning and unchanging moral principles. Immanuel Kant spoke for that absolutist ethical tradition when he argued that only knowledge that is absolutely certain can justify the abject obedience that moral law demands. He thought he had found a priori, rational grounds to justify the universal and unchanging character of moral law. Moral knowledge, he concluded, is a priori and certain. It tells us, for example, that murder, lying, and stealing are wrong. The fact that those acts may sometimes seem to benefit someone cannot diminish the absolute certainty that they are wrong. Thus, for example, it is a contradiction to state that murder can sometimes be right for, by its very nature, murder is wrong.

Most human rights are positive rights that involve the exploitation of resources. (Negative rights restrain governments and don't require resources. For example, governments shouldn't restrict our freedom of speech or tell us how to pray.) Wherever in the world a child is born, that child has all the inherent human rights—including the right to have food, housing, and medical care, which others must provide. When positive rights are accorded equally to everyone, they first allow and then support constant growth, of both population and the exploitation of natural resources.

There is a pragmatic refutation of the belief that moral knowledge is certain and infallible. If a growing population faces a scarcity of land and resources, an ethics of universal human rights with equality and justice for all will fail. Those who survive will inevitably live by a different ethics.

Once the resources necessary to satisfy total human needs become insufficient, options will be bracketed by two extremes. One is to ration resources so that everyone may share the inadequate supplies equally and justly.

The other extreme is to have people act like players in a game of musical chairs. In conditions of scarcity, there will be more people than chairs, so some people will be left standing when the music stops. Some—the self-sacrificing altruists—will refuse to take the food that others need and will perish. Others, however, will not play by the rules. Rejecting the ethics of a universal and unconditional moral law, they will fight to get the resources they need to live.

Under neither extreme, nor all the options in between, does it make sense to analyze the problem through the lens of human rights. The flaw in an ethical system of universal human rights, unqualified moral obligations, and equal justice for all can now be stated in its logically simplest form: If to try to live by those principles under conditions of scarcity causes it to be impossible to live at all, then the practice of that ethics will cease. Scarcity renders such formulations useless and ultimately causes such an ethics to become extinct. (Elliott and Lamm 2002)

We have described not a world that we want to see, but one that we fear might come to be. Human rights create moral obligations, and you can't have moral obligations to deliver the impossible, nor can humans have a moral duty to supply something if the act of supplying it harms the ecosystem to the point where life on earth becomes unsustainable. Moral codes, no matter how logical and well-reasoned, and human rights, no matter how compassionate, must make sense within the limitations of the ecosystem; we cannot disregard the factual consequences of our ethics. If acting morally compromises the ecosystem, then moral behavior must be rethought. Ethics cannot demand a level of resource use that the ecosystem cannot tolerate.

The consequences of human behavior change as the population grows. Most human activities have a point of moral reversal, before they may cause great benefit and little burden but after which they may cause harm to overwhelm any benefit. Here are a few representative examples, the first of which is often cited when considering Garrett Hardin's work.

First, in a nearly empty lifeboat, rescuing a drowning shipwreck victim causes benefit: It saves the life of the victim, and it adds another person to help manage the boat. But in a lifeboat loaded to the gunwales, rescuing another victim makes the boat sink and causes only harm: Everyone drowns.

Second, when the number of cars on a road is small, traveling by private car is a great convenience to all. But as the number of cars increases, a point of reversal occurs: The road now contains so many cars that such travel is inconvenient. The number of private cars may increase to the point where everyone comes to a halt. Thus, in some conditions, car travel benefits all. In other conditions, car travel makes it impossible for anyone to move; it can also pump so much carbon dioxide into the atmosphere that it alters the world's climate.

Third, economic growth can be beneficial when land, fuel, water, and other needed resources are abundant. But it becomes harmful when those resources become scarce or their exploitation causes ecological collapse. Every finite environment has a turning point at which further economic growth would produce so much trash and pollution that it would change from producing benefit to causing harm. After that point is reached, additional growth only increases scarcity and decreases overall productivity; in conditions of scarcity, economic growth has a negative impact.

Fourth, every environment is ultimately finite. Technology can extend but not eliminate limits. Only a few mature sugar maples survive on an acre of sugar bush; only so many radishes can grow in a five-foot row of dirt. Similar constraints operate in human affairs. When the population in any environment is small and natural resources are abundant, every additional person increases the welfare of all. As more and more people are added, they need increasingly to exploit the finite resources of that environment. At a certain point, the members of an increasing population become so crowded that they stop benefiting each other; by damaging the environment that supports everyone, by limiting the space available to each person, and by increasing the amount of waste and pollution, their activity begins to cause harm. That is, population growth changes from good to bad. And if the population continues to expand, its material demands may so severely damage the environment as to cause a tragedy of the commons—the collapse of both environment and society.

Those cases illustrate the fact that many activities are right—morally justified—when only a limited number of people do them. Yet the same activities become wrong—immoral—when populations increase and more and more resources are exploited.

Few people seem to understand the nature of steady growth. Any rate of growth has a doubling time—the period of time it takes for a given quantity to double. It is a logical inevitability—not a matter subject to debate—that it takes only a relatively few doublings for any given number, even a very small one, to equal or exceed any finite quantity, even a very large one.

Another way to look at the impact of growth is to think of a resource that would last one hundred years if people consumed it at a constant rate. If the rate of consumption increased 5 percent each year, the resource would last only thirty-six years. A supply adequate for one thousand years at a constant rate would last seventy-nine years at a 5-percent rate of growth; a ten-thousand-year supply would last only 125 years at the same rate. Just as no trees grow to the sky, no growth rate is ultimately sustainable. Because the natural resources available for human use are finite, exponential growth will use them up in a relatively small number of doublings. The only possible questions are those of timing: When will the resources be depleted beyond practical use? When will human society, which is now built on perpetual growth, fail?

The mathematics make it clear: Any human activity that uses matter or energy must reach a steady state (or a periodic cycle of boom and bust, which over the long run is the same thing). If not, it inevitably will cease to exist. The moral of the story is obvious: Any system of economics or ethics that requires or even allows steady growth in the exploitation of resources is destined to collapse; it is a recipe for disaster.

It is self-deception for anyone to believe that historical evidence contradicts mathematical necessity. The fact that the food supply since the time of Malthus has increased faster than the human population does not refute Malthus's general thesis: that an increasing population must, at some time, need more food, water, and other vital resources than the finite earth or creative technology can supply in perpetuity. In other words, the finitude of the earth makes it inevitable that any behavior causing growth in population or in the use of resources—including human moral, political, and economic behavior—will sooner or later be constrained by scarcity.

Unlike current ethics the ethics of the commons builds on the assumption of impending scarcity. Scarcity requires double-entry bookkeeping: Whenever someone gains goods or services that use matter or energy, someone else must lose matter or energy.

If the starving people of a distant nation get food aid from the United States, then the United States loses the same amount of the food as the needy people gain; it also loses the fertility of the soil that produced the food, loses the food it has sent abroad. To a point this is appropriate and workable; soon, however, helping one group of starving people may well mean that we cannot help others. Everything that a government does prevents it from doing something else. When you have to balance a budget, you can only say yes to some important services by saying no to others. Similarly, the ethics of the commons must rely on trade-offs not rights. It must specify who or what gains, and who or what loses.

Indeed, in a finite world full of mutually dependent beings, you never can do just one thing. Every human activity that uses matter or energy pulls with it a tangled skein of unexpected consequences. Conditions of crowding and scarcity can cause moral acts to change from causing benefit to causing harm, or even disaster; acts that once were moral can become immoral. We must constantly assess the complex of consequences, intended or not, to see if the overall benefit of seemingly moral acts outweighs their overall harm.

As Garrett Hardin suggested, the collapse of any common resource can be avoided only by limiting its use. The ethics of the commons builds on his idea that the best and most humane way of avoiding the tragedy of the commons is mutual constraint, mutually agreed on and mutually enforced.

Most important, the ethics of the commons must prevent a downward spiral to scarcity. One of its first principles must be that the human population must reach and maintain a stable state—a state in which population growth does not slowly but inexorably diminish the quality of, and even the prospect for, human life in the future. Another principle must be that human exploitation of natural resources remains safely below the maximum levels that a healthy and resilient ecosystem can sustain. A third must be to provide a margin of safety that prevents natural disasters like storms, floods, droughts, earthquakes, and volcanic eruptions from causing unsupportable scarcity.

Not to limit human behavior in accordance with those principles would be not only myopic, but also ultimately a moral failure. To let excess human fertility or excess demand for material goods and services cause a shortage of natural resources is as immoral as theft and murder, and for the same reasons: They deprive others of their property, the fruits of their labors, their quality of life, or even their lives.

The ethics of the commons is a pragmatic ethics. It denies the illusion that human moral behavior occurs in a never-never land, where human rights and duties remain unchanging and where scarcity can never cancel moral duties. It does not allow a priori moral arguments to dictate behavior that must inevitably become extinct. It accepts the necessity of constraints on both production and reproduction. As we learn how best to protect the health and endurance of the earth's ecosystems, the ethics of the commons can steadily make human life more worth living.

As populations increase and environments deteriorate, the moral laws and principles that humans have relied on so long can no longer solve the most pressing problems of the modern world. The ethics of the commons gives the needs and interests of an enduring and resilient environment moral precedence over human needs and interests. It requires that moral behavior work for the good of the whole as the means for securing human welfare. We cannot say, as the George H. W. Bush said in Rio in 1992 that the "American lifestyle is non-negotiable," but neither can we think in terms of "rights." Human rights are an inadequate and inappropriate basis to distribute scarce resources and new yardsticks must be proposed and debated.

Reform Party

I am very uncomfortable talking/thinking about my flirtation with the Reform Party. A good part of it because the party changed from a reform agenda to a right-wing agenda and from Ross Perot to Pat Buchanan. I do not want to be associated with either.

By the mid-1990s it became clear that neither political party was interested in taking on entitlements or running on a platform of fiscal responsibility. Deficit spending and debt was a Republican issue, if at all, and the Republicans ran from any sensible solution when they were in power. The public was largely unaware of the negative consequences of continuing to run large federal deficits. To be sure, AARP (the American

Association of Retired Persons) and public were very skeptical of any real attempts to reform entitlements or cut deficit spending.

HELLO PUBLIC! LISTEN UP! The government keeps its books the same way that a lemonade stand keeps its books: cash in/cash out. The federal government does not accrue its liabilities. The government publishes as a fact that the federal debt was $20 trillion, but this is a deception quite close to a lie. A corporation would be violating the law if it didn't disclose its full liabilities. We have locked in a great economic disruption that will soon explode. Most states have constitutional responsibilities to balance their budget—in other words, only spend what their income is. The federal government has no such restrictions and borrows money as needed.

If you ask what burden the current generation (us) has placed on future generations, a better answer would be $100 trillion, and trillions of dollars more in state and local obli-

LIFE IN THE MANSION

gations we have promised to pay. The real liability we are leaving our children is close to $150 trillion when it is all added up.

I believed then and still believe today that debt is going to cause a nation-threatening crisis and that neither political party can honestly address the issue. My generation and the one just before us learned to use public debt to allow us to live at the expense of those yet to be born or too young to object. We are now in a position similar to that described by the Roman historian Livy when he wrote, "We can neither bear our ills nor our cures." We are drifting toward a crisis, and we cannot do politically what we need to do economically to prevent this debt debacle. I felt so strongly about these issues that I wrote a heartfelt but inappropriate letter to Colorado congressman David Skaggs, one of the good guys, which was so vehement that it caused a rupture in our relationship.

Polls show only a plurality of voters favored the steps necessary to prevent this explosion. Hence, I thought, a new party running on fiscal reform could possibly achieve a plurality of voters and honestly fix the debt/entitlement crisis.

In 1995 and 1996 a group of us from around the country studied closely how a third party could be formed. It proved to be a gargantuan undertaking, but we noted with interest that Ross Perot had already spent tens of millions getting the Reform Party on the ballot. Perhaps we could take over this party already on most state ballots.

We even had proposed candidates: Senator John McCain for president and Senator Bob Kerry for vice president. Two Medal of Honor winners, one from each party. Neither of these senators said yes, but we thought if we could take over the Reform Party, they might be persuaded. At some point I sounded out Colin Powell too, but he quickly slammed the door. One in our group, Congressman Ed Zschau, agreed to run as vice president and I was persuaded to be the candidate for President.

It was quixotic but fun. I made a grand speech at our national convention at Valley Forge, Pennsylvania, and then got my head handed to be by the Perot delegates who had given me a standing ovation after my speech. Ross, who announced widely (and personally to me) that he wasn't going to run, immediately changed his mind and ran after all. I am convinced that he was never sincere about stepping aside, and I was naive to ever think that we would. He merely wanted to sucker someone into that race to create national interest, and that someone was me.

I remain convinced to this day that both political parties are captured and controlled by special interests, and that a new party or a new coalition must be formed from liberal Republicans and Democrats dedicated to compassionately putting our federal fiscal house in order. The task is beyond either of the existing parties with their special interests and can be done only by a plurality of voters, not a majority. We are approaching a historic testing point of democracy to successfully make hard choices.

HARRY TRUMAN

Before I moved to Denver, My friend Phil Hammer and I went to Washington, D.C., hoping to land jobs in the Department of Justice. As we drove east, we just happened to stop for gas in Independence, Missouri. The man who was pumping my gas (yes, that is the way they used to do it) started a conversation that pressed a mental button, and I asked him, "Doesn't Harry Truman live here?" "Hell yes," he responded, "he lives ten blocks south." On a whim, I pointed my car south and soon sat the bottom of his sidewalk. A fairly large white house stood before me, surrounded by a fence and gate—but a neighbor-friendly fence, one that was easily accessible. "Success is the child of audacity," I thought, and I went up and knocked on the door.

A man in a sport coat answered, and I told him I was a newly minted lawyer and wondered if I could pay my respects to the president. He invited me into the foyer and asked me to wait. It turns out that at that time Truman had refused Secret Service protection, and, I learned later, he only reluctantly accepted security after the Kennedy assassination. The man who was on duty when I knocked was an Independence, Missouri detective, furnished at the expense of the city of Independence.

Five minutes later, here came President Truman, dressed in a coat and tie. We chatted for what could not have been more than four minutes, and then I suddenly knew I was dismissed. Body language, I suspect. But the fact that he would take the time to greet a nobody who simply knocked on his door taught me a great lesson. I always tried to accommodate and greet people when they asked, and I seek out people I notice who want to say hello but are hesitant to ask.

GOVERNOR GLOOM

Life has been good to me. Extraordinarily good. I am healthy, my family is healthy, and my kids and grandkids all live in Denver. I am happily married to a wonderful, wonderful woman and have succeeded beyond my talents. So why am I gloomy? Why do I view the world through the lens of a pessimist?

I believe I am gloomy for valid reasons, and that all thoughtful people ought to have some degree of gloom as they look at the world around them. I am haunted by the world I am leaving my kids and grandkids. I inherited the world's largest creditor nation, and I am leaving them the world's largest debtor nation. The largest debtor nation in history. I inherited an exporting nation, and I am leaving my kids an importing nation with the largest trade deficit in world history. My mother and father fought a war and a depression and left me with just a small federal debt, yet I am leaving my children a debt of $55 to $150 trillion dollars, which is more than the total private wealth in America and which would take five or six years of their total wages to pay off. We have significantly "pre-spent" our children's money.

I inherited an America that produced more than it consumed, and I am leaving an America that consumes more than it produces. I inherited a spending-and-investing society, and I am leaving a spending-and-borrowing society. I inherited a world of delayed gratification, and I am leaving a world of instant gratification. Violent crime has gone up 560 percent, the divorce rate 400 percent, and there has been an eighty-point drop in the SAT.

But my greatest guilt is leaving my children and grandchildren a world with a planet-destroying warming trend that will heavily impact, if not destroy their lives. We are traveling on an environmental *Titanic*. We talk about "saving the earth," but that is not technically correct. The earth will survive whether or not we act on global warming and the other megaissues. Ninety-nine percent of all species in geologic time have become extinct, yet the earth survives. Ice ages, warming ages, cataclysmic challenges of many types have come and gone and the earth survives. I want to save the earth for humans to continue to survive and thrive. I want my grandchildren and their children (and your children and grandchildren) to have a livable earth.

BILL SIGNING IN THE GOVERNOR'S OFFICE

You become what you focus on, and I focus on public policy. Truth be told I am a public policy junkie. When I reflect why this is, it becomes crystal-ball clear. It was John F. Kennedy who got me interested in the political world.

I was in my second year at Berkeley when John F. Kennedy was running for president (1960), and I was caught up in what later became known as Camelot. I was a typical child of the 1950s, indifferent to and ignorant of public policy. But John F. Kennedy somehow ignited a spark across the nation. Young, idealistic, a war hero, he spoke to our souls. We wanted to build a more just, more compassionate America. Yes, we were naive, but that is not a venal sin. The first campaign I ever walked door-to-door in was JFK's 1960 campaign. We won. Happy days were here again.

But that experience set the bar. We could be X and instead we are $-X$. My generation could/should have eliminated the debt, but instead we doubled it, then doubled it again, then doubled it again, and then two more doublings. We didn't help the underclass much; instead we added a second underclass through our dysfunctional immigration system.

So, I am gloomy first because I am a professor of public policy and spend my time focusing on public policy, and second because there is a Grand-Canyon gap between the world I intended to leave to the next generation and what I am actually leaving. But could there be a third reason? Could we actually be heading into a time of economic and environmental chaos? We tend to forget that Cassandra was right.

I have spent a great deal of time and effort fighting for us to recognize and correct the fiscal mess we have made for our children. It isn't here yet, but it is coming. I believe that a good part of the prosperity of my generation has been stolen from our children. And I see a new issue forming, intergenerational equity, which will have a harsh judgment of my generation's time in power. My generation borrowed heavily from the next generation, but for consumption, not investment. We started borrowing, and then borrowing became a way of life and a regular political practice. We borrowed as if we could borrow forever, but economics teaches us we cannot. There are always pipers to be paid!

6. TEN COMMANDMENTS OF COMMUNITY

COURAGE

Men are taught early on to evidence courage, and that this is the mark of a man. "Step aside and let the women and children into the life-boats." In reality, the world is brimming with strong women. Consider the settlement of the American West, which is filled with stories of courage by women who were also better survivors than their male counterparts. Just look at the Donner Party: half of the party died, but significantly more women survived than men. I often reflected on the issue of courage in my early life. Would I rise to the occasion if confronted with a situation that required courage?

As it happened, two incidents occurred when I was fifteen that reflected on my innate courage. The first was when I was a Boy Scout in Pittsburgh, Pennsylvania. I was on an overnight winter camping trip to a Boy Scout camp, two hours from Pittsburgh. I was helping to do the dishes near my tent, when two of my fellow scouts ran up and said that three of our troop had fallen through the ice. I ran to the lake and there I saw, out toward the middle of the lake, a boy struggling to get up out of the water. Only one boy, but I had been told three fell through the ice. By the time I got to the shore of the lake, ten or fifteen other boys stood with me watching, but no one was making a move to help. I don't remember even weighing the decision to act, I just started walking out on the ice. The ice cracked and groaned all around me as I tiptoed past the one wet and cold boy crawling toward shore. I could see a second boy emerging from the ice, struggling to get out of the watery grave and onto the ice.

He had made it out by the time I got to the open water, and I asked him about the other boy. "He's still in there," the boy responded. Then, operating on instinct, I took off my shoes and coat and jumped in. Wham! I knew I had limited time in the water, and it chilled me to the bone on first contact. I dove down and immediately looked up to position the gap in the ice and map my escape route. I then looked around me in the murky water trying to spot the missing boy. No luck, so back to the surface for a big breath and then down again. No luck again, but on this third dive I knew I was in trouble. I was cold and incredibly numb. The water was cloudy and I did a final 360-degree turn, trying to spot the boy. I suspect he was within ten feet of me, but I had no clue which direction. I knew I had to get out fast. Getting out of a hole in the ice is no small task, but I was able to pull myself out and then crawl back to shore where I was met by our troop leader who took me back to camp where there was a fire and warm, dry clothes.

The sheriff's department found the boy's body later that afternoon. The sheriff later took me aside told me that I had done a very brave but very foolish thing. "We almost had two dead boys," he told me. This message was also conveyed to me by my troop leader, and later by my proud but horrified parents. "What would you have done if you found him?" the sheriff lectured, and of course he was right. I was clearly guilty of bad judgment, but was I brave? To this day I don't know. Many brave acts start off as misjudgments. In my own eyes I had done a stupid thing, but I was also secretly proud. I had not done nothing, I had acted.

The second episode was also in 1951, when our parents took us to Acapulco, Mexico, for a vacation. It was a great trip, with two days in Mexico City to see the Chapultepec Castle, the Aztec temples, and the floating gardens.

The second day in Acapulco, already bored (I am not much of a beach person), my brother Tom and I took surfboards and kayak paddles and made our way out into the bay. I mean way, way out into the bay. We had barely begun our return when my paddle broke. Here we were, far out in the bay, and me with a broken paddle. I remember being immediately apprehensive. No, in all honesty—scared. We could hardly see the shore, and I could not see the resort from where we had first embarked.

We started toward shore. I was using my hands, but Tom with his intact kayak paddle was the only one making any progress. And by this time, the tide had turned against us. Tom was eleven or twelve years old at that time and in good shape. He could've as easily been the one to paddle for help. But I took his paddle: "Here, Tom, give me the paddle and I will go for help," said I from a four-year advantage in age. Tom trustfully gave me his paddle, and off I went back to shore, leaving my adored brother drifting out to sea with my broken paddle.

Tom in his magnanimous way never blamed me and seemed to take it as a given that the older brother should've been the one to go for help. Of course, I did get successfully to shore and told the lifeguard, who in turn got a boat, and the boatman, the lifeguard, and I went to rescue Tom.

I mull on this event often over the years. I do know that I was scared and thought of myself first. To this day Tom thinks nothing of it, but I remember my guilt and relief when our rescue boat approached his bobbing head. We were safe, but in my own eyes (to this day), I had not acted honorably.

One of my most successful speeches and topics is the question of how diverse people live together in peace. I recognized from the beginning that I could only scratch the surface, but I felt raising the subject was important. It touches on many of the themes that I have been so passionate about. How do we all get along in this fast-moving, diverse society? I have given a variation of this speech hundreds of time, both within and outside of Colorado. Here is an early version.

I believe there are many new tensions pulling at the American community. We are getting more diverse all the time, and the melting pot in places is becoming a pressure cooker. From 20 to 25 percent of people in California, New York, and New Jersey are foreign born (8.6 percent in Colorado). We have geographic, political, generational, racial, and ethnic divisions all tending to pull us apart. Perhaps it is time to go to our original roots and look anew at what community is—and what it means.

A great writer once said: "The real voyage of discovery consists not in seeking new lands, but in seeing with new eyes." Let us look with "new eyes" at community. What is community?

A community is much more than a place on a map. It is a state of mind, shared values, shared vision, a common fate. A diverse community is not a state of nature. A "herd" is a state of nature, a "flock," a "covey," a "gaggle" is a state of nature, but alas—not a community. A community of different religions, races, and nationalities is against most of the lessons of history, as we see daily on our TV sets. Humans bond to families, but not necessarily with their neighbors. A community requires a unique set of skills: social architects, bridge builders, and structural engineers who build bonds, bridges, who remove barriers. It needs shared customs, traditions, values, principles, and institutions.

Denver, Colorado is by definition a place on the map, but it is not intrinsically a community. A community is not geography—it is not who lives in an area—it is the web of human relationships of the people who live in a particular place. As every house is not a home, every spot on the map is not a com-

CARRYING THE OLYMPIC TORCH

munity. Houses shelter, homes nurture. Communities nurture. Communities are forged by commitment, dedication, hard work, tolerance, love, and a search for commonalties. Our forefathers and foremothers built a community and passed it on to us, but it is not like the South Platte River or Mount Evans, which we will inevitably pass on to our children. We will not inevitably pass community to our children. Community is not a guarantee; it is a continuing challenge.

September 11 tested community, and most of us are proud of how America responded to the challenge. But the real test lies ahead. Community is a no-brainer when a nation is attacked. Robert Maynard Hutchins observed, "The death of democracy is not likely to be an assassination from ambush. It will be a slow extinction from apathy, indifference and undernourishment." Another wise woman talked about the danger of "subversive inactivity," meaning that if we don't participate in our civic society, if 50 percent of us don't even vote, that is more dangerous than "subversive activity." We have to care enough about our democracy and community to keep it nurtured, and we have to do it year after year.

Given all these new geopolitical, economic, and social realities we must ask: How do we define and build a quality, sustainable community? This is an immensely important question. We see daily the results of not building a community:

- In Bosnia and Kosovo
- In Chechnya
- In Sri Lanka
- In Quebec and Northern Ireland
- In Rwanda
- In Afghanistan
- In Myanmar

What is going on today in former Yugoslavia, Miramar and Chechnya is not a failure of communism. It is failure of community. The Albanians, Serbs, Slovenians, Croats, and Bosnians were killing each other before Marx was born. The people in Bosnia are far less diverse than in the United States—the secret is that we formed a community (e pluribus unum) and Bosnia did not.

People who share a geographic area must become a community—or they become Balkanized, fragmented, and fractionalized. We all bond naturally to our families; we bond to our geographic location:

"If you don't know where you are, you don't know who you are," says another well-known poet.

But, we do not bond easily to our neighbors. We seem to instinctively view them as competitors. A community needs a shared stake in the future. It needs a shared language, shared culture, shared norms and values. It needs, in short, social glue that is the essence of community. It must understand that all members to a certain degree have a shared fate. To say my fate is not tied to your fate is like saying, "Your end of the boat is sinking."

We must give more thought and discussion to those things that build community—that hold us together as a community— and how to minimize those factors that separate us—like race, religion, and ethnicity. Diversity carried too far is divisiveness.

I should, thus, like to give you TEN COMMANDMENTS OF COMMUNITY—ten building blocks that I believe are imperative as we try to renew and expand our sense of community.

COMMANDMENT I: DO NOT TAKE COMMUNITY FOR GRANTED. COMMUNITY MUST BE CONSTANTLY REGENERATED, REVITALIZED, AND RENEWED.

Too many Americans believe that God is an American who will watch over us no matter how diverse we become, or how hedonistic, selfish, myopic, or inefficient we become.

This is a dangerous hubris. No great nation in history has ever withstood the ravages of time. Arnold Toynbee warns us that all great nations rise and all fall, and that the "autopsy of history is that all great nations commit suicide." God will not automatically save America. With God's help, we must save ourselves.

We cannot rely on past success to ensure future success, and we cannot take the future for granted. Successful communities—successful countries—don't just happen. They are built by dedication, sacrifice, and hard work. They must find or build unifying bonds and values. They also are built by caring for each other, helping each other, and working jointly on projects and programs.

A great Amazon legend gives us a metaphor for cooperation and community: it tells of a priest who was speaking with God about heaven and hell. "I will show you hell," said God. They went into a room that had a delicious beef stew on the table, around which sat people chained to their benches and who looked desperately famished. They held spoons with long handles that reached into the pot, but were too long to put the stew back into their mouths. Their suffering was terrible. "Now, I will show you heaven," said God. They then went into an identical room with the savory stew on the table, around which sat people with identical spoons and handles, but they were well nourished and joyous. The priest was baffled until God said, "Quite simply, you see, these people have learned to feed each other."

We can create chaos, as in Bosnia, or we can create community. It is up to us.

COMMANDMENT II: A GREAT COMMUNITY NEEDS GREAT LEADERS, BUT MORE IMPORTANTLY, IT NEEDS GREAT CITIZENS.

Leadership is important. We all know this. Winston Churchill said, "An army of lions led by sheep will always lose to an army of sheep led by a lion." But citizens are equally important.

America, in many respects, faces more of a "participation" problem than a leadership problem. One wise historian observed:

> To make a nation truly great, a handful of heroes capable of great deeds at supreme moments is not enough. Heroes are not always available, and one can often do without them! But it is essential to have thousands of reliable people—honest citizens—who steadfastly place the public interest before their own.
>
> —Pasquale Villani

John Gardner, former secretary of the Department of Health and Human Services, similarly warns:

> Our society cannot achieve greatness unless individuals at many levels of ability accept the need for high standards of performance and strive to achieve those standards within the limits possible for them. We want the highest conceivable excellence, of course, in the activities crucial to our effectiveness and creativity as a society, but that isn't enough. If the man in the street says, "Those fellows at the top have to be good, but I'm just a slob and can act like one"—then our days of greatness are behind us.

A quality community needs more than leadership; it needs quality citizens. Men and women like the firefighters and police officers at the World Trade Center. Danger was nothing to them, courage, duty, and honor everything, serving their community regardless of danger to themselves. A total 388 firefighters lost their lives, but 30,000 people escaped before the towers fell in large part because of the sacrifice of these 388. What an eloquent statement of community that was!

A quality community can only be built on the bedrock of quality citizens, who have a stake in their neighbors and give of themselves.

COMMANDMENT III: A COMMUNITY MUST GENERATE
TOLERANCE AND YET SET LIMITS ON THAT TOLERANCE.
IT MUST BALANCE FREEDOM WITH SOCIAL ORDER, RIGHTS
WITH RESPONSIBILITIES, AUTONOMY WITH COMMUNITY.

We have been given the greatest inheritance (patrimony) from
what Tom Brokaw called "The Greatest Generation": social
and political stability. They left us freedom, but more than that
an equilibrium between freedom and order—a first rate infrastructure, small national debt, and a tradition of barn raising
and tolerance.

Tolerance is a word easy to say—hard to apply. What
should the community tolerate and what shouldn't it tolerate?
It often depends on context. It is your right to read your Bible,
your Koran, your Torah. It is not your right to force these
readings on others. We can tolerate almost any idea, and the
community should be alive with argument.

But the standards for teaching and tolerance are not
coterminous. It may be that you deeply believe that it's trees
moving that make the wind blow. This is your prerogative, but
you cannot teach it to my children in public institutions. You
can stage debates in your school between Republicans and
Democrats because their differences are open to debate and
constantly changing, but you do not give equal time in schools
to how trees moving make the wind blow. Science and rational
thought have put to rest certain arguments, and knowledge
must move forward if we are to survive in a competitive world.
We can tolerate many private beliefs, but should stand strong
against institutionalizing non-science and scientific error into
our school system.

There are some people who believe the Holocaust never
happened. They are entitled to be mistaken—even gravely
mistaken. They can stand on a soapbox on Main Street and
profess that there was no Holocaust—but they cannot teach in
our schools a viewpoint that all evidence points against. We
have pictures of concentration camps and Holocaust victims.

And, we have pictures in rocks (called fossils), which show us the inspiring story of evolution. Schools must struggle with knowledge, but cannot teach a particular theology—or all minority viewpoints no matter how passionately held.

Even more important is tolerance in the area of behavior, especially where behavior does not hurt others, and/or where no societal consensus exists. What should a community made up of various races, religions, and ethnic groups tolerate and what should it not tolerate? The late Barbara Jordan talked about the need to "Americanize" immigrants. How tolerant should our society be and what should we demand of immigrants from other cultures who come here with vastly different ideas of individualism, constitutionalism, human rights, equality, liberty, rule of law, democracy, separation of church and state, private property? How many conflicting, contrasting, and overlapping cultures can live together in peace and harmony? What happens when a separatist culture clashes with a pluralist culture? When "Why can't we all just get along?" meets "There is no God but Allah"?

Certainly there should be freedom of religion, but can people handle snakes, refuse medical care, and refuse on religious grounds to salute the flag? People can refuse a blood transfusion for themselves and even all medical care if they want. We have generally allowed people to do these things on grounds of their religion. In fact, I saw a bumper sticker the other day that read, "I've just become a Christian Scientist, it was the only health plan I could afford."

But should they be allowed to refuse medical care for their minor children, can they force their thirteen-year-old daughter to marry her forty-five-year old uncle, or submit to female genital mutilation? Should Muslim clerics have the right to broadcast over outdoor loudspeakers the five daily Islamic calls to prayer? Should we give in to demands of some Muslim clerics for publicly maintained prayer facilities in such institutions as schools and airports? Should a Muslim woman be able to get her driver's license picture taken while in purdah?

Does the state have to maintain kosher kitchens in its prison system? Or can Hispanic students demand a separate graduation where the Mexican, not the American, flag is flown? Should the ritual slaughter of animals be forbidden under our animal rights laws? Do we grant a zoning variance to allow a mosque to build a prayer tower? Should Sikhs be allowed to wear their daggers, so central to their religion, on airplanes? Louisiana cockfighters are suing the federal government over a new ban on shipping fighting birds, saying it is discrimination against Cajuns and Hispanics. They claim that the ban is "moral imperialism" and that cockfighting is integral to their culture. All these examples challenge us to think about the limits to tolerance and multiculturalism.

Certainly there can and should be some reasonable accommodation to diversity. Someone in our public hospitals can't refuse to be treated by a Black or Jewish doctor? We say no. But how about our Muslim immigrants for whom their religion forbids another man from seeing or touching the body of a wife/woman? Why not allow her request a woman doctor for reasons of public health? But we are not going to let her perform female genital mutilation on her twelve-year-old daughter.

Finding a balance between tolerance and chaos, rights and privileges, freedom and community will always be a work in progress.

COMMANDMENT IV: A COMMUNITY CAN BE A JOSEPH'S COAT OF MANY COLORS AND CREEDS, BUT IT MUST HAVE MORE THINGS IN COMMON THAN DIFFERENCES. IT MUST STRESS THE "UNUM," NOT THE PLURIBUS."

Diversity is a word sweeping America and, in particular, sweeping college campuses. It is appropriate to "celebrate diversity," but I suggest we must celebrate unity even more. I recently went around the world and in no place, with the possible exception of the United States, did I see "diversity" working. Diverse people worldwide are mostly engaged in hating each other—that is, when they are not killing each other. A "diverse," peaceful, or stable society is against most historical precedent. It cannot be achieved with slogans or happy talk. It is much harder to achieve than most Americans acknowledge. A nation is not a rooming house where we all live separately while we make our livings. I believe that a society can be a Joseph's coat of many diverse people, but they absolutely must have more in common than what separates them. We must share something with our neighbors besides a zip code.

I am sobered by how much unity it takes. Look at the ancient Greeks. Dorf's *World History* tells us:

> The Greeks believed that they belonged to the same race; they possessed a common language and literature; and they worshiped the same gods. All Greece took part in the Olympic games in honor of Zeus and all Greeks venerated the shrine of Apollo at Delphi. A common enemy Persia threatened their liberty. Yet, all of these bonds together were not strong enough to overcome two factors ... (local patriotism and geographical conditions that nurtured political divisions...).

Our culture doesn't have to be (and shouldn't be) the culture of 1776 or 1950—but it must have a unified core. The United States runs the very great risk of creating a "Hispanic Quebec" if we do not develop the right "social glue." As Benjamin Schwarz said in *The Atlantic Monthly* back in 1995:

> The apparent success of our own multiethnic and multicultural experiment might have been achieved not by tolerance but by hegemony. Without the dominance that once dictated ethnocentrically, and what it meant to be an American, we are left with only tolerance and pluralism to hold us together. (Schwarz) observes, "Americanization" was a process of coercive conformi-

ty according to which the U.S. was a melting pot, not
a tapestry. We took immigrants and turned them into
Americans. (Schwarz 1995)

Tolerance and pluralism are not enough. The history of
multiple cultures living together without assimilation is not a
happy history. Another scholar bluntly put it this way: "Ameri-
canization, then, although it did not cleanse America of its
ethnic minorities, it cleansed its minorities of their ethnicity."
Blunt but true. We took Irish, Indians and Italians, Cambodians
and Chinese, Europeans and Ethiopians and made them into
Americans. A nation must be more than a diverse people living
in the same place and sharing only a standard of living.

There are three factors that begin with *D* that helped
America assimilate. The first is *Distance*. Immigrants came
from a long distance and often couldn't go home. They had
to become Americans. Today, a substantial percentage of
our immigrants can go home for the weekend. The second is
Diversity. Immigrants came from so many different places that
they had to learn a common language to communicate. Today,
almost 70 percent of our immigrants come from Spanish-
speaking countries, and, for example, you can live your whole
live in west Denver and never speak English. The third is
Discontinuity, where times of large immigration were followed
by wars or depression that virtually stopped immigration and
allowed those here to assimilate. (Thanks, Sam Huntington, for
the concept of the "three Ds"). Today, we take unprecedented
numbers of immigrants, and we do so year after year. America
faces a new and serious assimilation challenge.

I thus suggest that diversity is only an asset if it is second-
ary to unity. The emphasis must be on the "unum," not the
"pluribus." We can be composed of many ethnic groups and
religions, but we must be one nationality. We should respect
diversity, but we should celebrate unity.

COMMANDMENT V: A COMMUNITY WILL REMAIN A
COMMUNITY ONLY AS LONG AS IT HAS JUSTICE AND
HONORS PEACEFUL CHANGE.

There is nothing more important to community than justice.
People must feel that they are fairly treated and that when
justice is administered it is even-handed and proportionate. If I
don't spend a lot of time recounting here the reasons justice is
needed, it is not that it isn't important, but that it is obvious.

A community needs institutions to mediate individual
and group differences. That includes both substantive justice
and procedural justice. A community must be to some degree
self-governing. Community needs citizens, not subjects, but
it needs citizens who recognize and honor democratic institutions. We must believe more in the bloodless revolution we call

CONFERRING WITH PRESIDENT JIMMY CARTER

"elections" than who
wins the election. As
one thoughtful person
wrote: "A democratic
community enjoying
political liberty is
only possible when
the attachment of the
majority of citizens
to political liberty is
stronger than their
attachment to specific
political doctrines."
(Conquest 2000)

Some institution must engender enough loyalty and authority to prevail when interests and factions conflict. Many people
see public schools as wellsprings of civic virtue. That discussion takes more time than we have here.

What a lesson we have had in loyalty to community in
the 2000 presidential election. We didn't need to like, or even
agree with the Florida voting procedures or the US Supreme

Court decision to accept them. Our attachment to democracy was greater than our partisanship. Amitai Etzioni says democracy is where we all fight with one arm tied behind our backs.

COMMANDMENT VI: A QUALITY COMMUNITY IS ONE THAT ANTICIPATES THE FUTURE.

A community must care about and anticipate its future. Citizens must anticipate major changes that will take place in their society. It must foresee and forestall. Public policy is like a kaleidoscope, and time turns it to present us with whole new patterns. Let me discuss a couple of possibly community-damaging issues we face. The first is the "aging of America."

America is getting older—fast. In 1900, we could expect to live 47.3 years; by 2017, the average male could expect to reach the age of seventy-six and the average female eighty-one. It is likely those born early this century can expect to live to eighty-five. In 1900, only 4.1 percent of Americans were over the age of 65. Today, over 13 percent are over the age of sixty-five. Yet, by the year 2030, it is likely that 20 percent, or 1 in 5, will be 65 or older. It may go even higher. The over-sixty-five population for the last fifty years has been growing four times faster than the rest of the population. The United States today has more people over the age of sixty-five than Canada has people. In the next forty years, we will add more than 40 million people over sixty-five to the thirty-one million we presently have. This is essentially adding yet another Canada, plus all the people in the Rocky Mountain states to our elderly population.

"This is the first time humans have altered the age structure of the population," says University of Chicago demographer Jay Olshansky. Sam Preston estimates that more than two-thirds of the improvement in longevity, from prehistoric times to the present, has taken place in the twentieth century.

We are not only increasing the number and percentage of elderly, but the elderly themselves are getting older as modern medicine performs its miracles and a larger percentage of our population lives beyond seventy-five. The fastest growing demographic cohort in the United States is people over one hundred; the second fastest growing cohort is people over eighty-five. These two trends have a great impact on the general demographic growth of the twentieth century. Since 1900, the population of the United States has tripled. The population of those over sixty-five grew ten times, and the population of those over eighty-five grew thirty times. This trend will continue. More than 10 percent of the elderly have at least one child who is over sixty-five. These realities will push us into uncharted territory for public policy.

Extended longevity is clearly good news for us individually. Eighty percent of babies born today will live past their sixty-fifth birthday, while fifty years ago fewer than 40 percent lived to see their sixty-fifth birthday. Today's senior citizens have unprecedented and wonderful opportunities for a dignified and active retirement.

But public policy views this with mixed emotions. Compounding the increase in life expectancy and the sheer number of elderly is a third demographic revolution taking place: the drop in the birthrate. People age from the moment they are born, but societies do not automatically age. Societies age mainly by a drop in the birthrate and an increase in longevity. This is what is happening in America and much of the world. In 1957, the American woman, on average, would bear 3.8 children. Today, she has 2.0. Twenty percent of the baby boomers have no children, and 25 percent will have only one. During the last half century, an extraordinarily large generation was followed by an extraordinarily small generation. The average American adult has more living parents than children. Since 1983, for the first time in history, America has more people over sixty-five than it has teenagers and more people over eighty-five than under five. It is this higher proportion of both elderly and "old old" (over eighty-five) that so compounds the challenges facing an aging society.

Soon America will be a vastly different society. Allan Pifer and Lydia Bronte observe:

> By the middle of the next century, when this revolution has run its course, the impacts will have been at least as powerful as that of any of the great economic and social movements of the past—movements such as the conquest and subsequent closing of the frontier, the successive waves of European immigration, the development of our great cities, or from more recent times, the post–WWII baby boom, the civil rights and women's movements, the massive influx of women into the paid labor force, the revolution in sexual mores, and the decay of many of our large urban centers. All these developments have had a profound effect on our nation, but the aging of the population will certainly have an equal, if not greater impact. (Pifer and Bronte 1986)

The United States is not alone in this demographic challenge. Worldwide, approximately five hundred million people, 9 percent of the present population, are age sixty or above. The World Bank warns that "the world faces a looming old age crisis," and it estimates that, by 2030, individuals over age sixty will number 1.5 billion, making up 16 percent of the population. The problem will be particularly acute for developed countries where pension funds are headed toward bankruptcy under this demographic avalanche.

The results of this demographic change are in some ways predictable, in others, unknowable. Without change in the current trends, America in 2050 will be a very different place.

Very high proportions of elderly persons and very high dependency ratios accompanied by continuing low fertility and very low mortality could have profound social and economic consequences. Education, health care, housing, recreation, and work life would be affected by the changes in age structure described. There could be severe dislocations in the economy as it tries to adjust to the changing needs for jobs, goods, and services. Tax rates could become oppressively high and serve as a disincentive to work. Younger workers will be called on for larger and larger financial contributions to the federal treasury on behalf of older nonworkers.

In all cultures, in all nations, and in all religions, there is a universal theme against profligacy and urging justice for future generations. A community cares about posterity. An old Middle East proverb observes, "The beginning of wisdom comes when a person plants a tree, the shade under which he knows he will never sit." Wise words.

COMMANDMENT VII: A GREAT COMMUNITY IS ONE THAT HAS DEVELOPED A GREAT COMMUNITY CULTURE.

We need a community culture, which gives diverse people a stake in each other. A community can celebrate differences, but they must have a certain level of trust in each other and feel some sense of commitment toward each other. A community must have things they do or honor in common: voting, volunteering, donating blood, attending town meetings, trusting their neighbors and coworkers. There has to be a substantial degree of "civic engagement" in community and some common loyalties.

America has come a long way since we questioned electing a Catholic president and a Black president. It is thus not even a stretch to imagine a woman, or a Latino, elected president before the century grows much older. Harlan Cleveland, the ambassador to NATO under President Lyndon Johnson, challenges us to "try to imagine a Turkish Chancellor of Germany, an Algerian President of France, a Pakistani Prime Minister of Britain, a Christian President of Egypt, an Arab Prime Minister of Israel, a Jewish President of Syria, a Tibetan running China and anyone but a Japanese in power in Tokyo."

I think more and more about "social capital" and community culture these days. Social capital is where people work together to solve problems, and have a habit of trusting each other and working out their problems peacefully. A great community is one that has developed a great community culture. James Fallows puts it this way: "In the long run, a society's strength depends on the way that ordinary people voluntarily behave."

A successful community culture encourages certain traits:

- Citizen participation
- Community leadership
- Volunteerism and philanthropy
- Civic education
- Community pride
- Justice

When Alexis de Tocqueville visited America in the 1830s he observed:

> These Americans are a peculiar people. If, in a local community, a citizen becomes aware of a human need, which is not being met, he thereupon discusses the situation with his neighbors. Suddenly a committee comes into existence. The committee thereupon begins to operate on behalf of the need and a new community function is established. It is like a miracle because these citizens perform this act without a single reference to any bureaucracy or any official agency.

He goes on to compare how Europe and America solve problems. He suggests that giving, volunteering, and joining are mutually reinforcing and habit forming, what Tocqueville called "habits of the heart." In Europe, he said, they would wait for the king or prince or government to fix it. In America, he observed people would form an association and solve the problem themselves.

A community must have adequate "social capital." Whereas physical capital is our physical infrastructure: roads, bridges, and water systems, "social capital" is the social networks: the habits of neighborliness and patriotism, the trust we developed with working and relating to others. It is the whole network of reciprocal social relations.

Societies run on reciprocity to some extent. Yogi Berra once said, "If you don't go to people's funerals, they won't go to yours." Successful communities have successful community cultures. Winston Churchill said: "We build our buildings and then they build us.

Likewise, we build our community culture and then it builds us.

COMMANDMENT VIII: A COMMUNITY NEEDS A STRONG COLLECTIVE IDENTITY, INCLUDING A SHARED CULTURE AND A SHARED LANGUAGE.

John Gardner says:

> If the community is lucky, and fewer and fewer are, it will have a shared history and tradition. It will have its "story," its legends and heroes, and will retell that story often. It will have symbols of group identity—a name, a flag, a location, songs and stories ... which it will use to heighten its members' sense of belonging.

He goes on to say:

> To maintain the sense of belonging and the dedication and commitment so essential to community life, members need inspiring reminders of shared goals and values. (Gardner 1990)

I am convinced that one of the "shared values" we must have is a shared language. It is a blessing for an individual to be bilingual—it is a curse for a society to be bilingual. We need a common currency so we can pay our debts to each other in understandable form, and we must be able to articulate our differences and celebrate our commonalties. Societies must be able to talk to each other. One scholar, Seymour Martin Lipset, put it this way:

> The histories of bilingual and bicultural societies that do not assimilate are histories of turmoil, tension, and tragedy. Canada, Belgium, Malaysia, Lebanon—all face crises of national existence in which minorities press for autonomy, if not independence. Pakistan and Cyprus have divided. Nigeria suppressed an ethnic rebellion. France faces difficulties with its Basques, Bretons, and Corsicans. (Boulding, Kammen and Lipset 1978)

The United States, in my opinion, is at a crossroads. It must move toward either greater integration or toward more fragmentation. It will either have to assimilate much better all of the peoples within its boundaries, or it will see an increasing alienation and fragmentation. Bilingual and bicultural nations are inherently unstable. We found in the 1950s that "separate was inherently unequal." But, we must also find that separate is also inherently divisive.

COMMANDMENT IX: THOU SHALL NOT ASK WHAT YOUR COMMUNITY CAN DO FOR YOU. THOU SHALL ASK WHAT YOU CAN DO FOR YOUR COMMUNITY.

A quality community is one that balances rights and privileges with duties and responsibilities. No society can live on rights and privileges alone, and we have tried too long. Our community and our nation—which nurtured us—now needs something in return. A community must demand some duties and responsibilities from its citizens. We must ask, "What we can do for our community?"

Just as a boat needs a sail and an anchor, a community needs freedom and some restriction on that freedom. *Freedom* is a wonderful word, but it does not trump all other considerations.

Saul Bellow postulates that "America is as threatened by an excess of liberty as Russia was by the absence of liberty." Those are important words. An eighteenth-century philosopher put it another way: "Freedom is the luxury of self-discipline." "America, the Beautiful" mirrors that same thought when it says: "Confirm thy soul in self-control by liberty and law."

A free republic demands a far higher degree of virtue than any earlier society. It demands a profound sense of personal responsibility, a willingness to govern one's own passions, a capacity for initiative and self-reliance, a taste for personal independence, and a sustained spirit of civic cooperation.

In short, tolerance in moderation becomes a safety net. Tolerance stretched too far becomes an apathetic vacuum where the holes are larger than the strings are strong—a vacuum that invites the criminals and the narrow moralists rather than the truly moral to rush in.

We cannot ever pass enough laws and ordinances to substitute for a sense of civic virtue. Communities need standards as well as laws. Admiral Nelson, off of Trafalgar, hoisted these words: "England expects every man to do his duty." And so must every woman; and yes, every child old enough to feed a younger brother or sister with a long spoon.

COMMANDMENT X:

I shall not give you a tenth commandment. I give you a challenge instead. I have missed important elements of community. What else is needed for community? Let us have a dialogue right now.

Conclusion

An old Presbyterian hymn out of my youth says: "New occasions teach new duties. Time makes ancient good uncouth."

Community is both an ancient and modern "good." But we can no longer take "community" for granted in the United States. We have too much evidence that we are unraveling and becoming unglued. There is too much tension, too much misunderstanding. Too many separate tribes yelling at each other. Our civic dialogue is too often a "dialogue" between the blind and the deaf. It is dangerous and we must attempt to salvage that elusive concept of community.

But at the same time the American community is strong and productive... It has survived war, depression, and civil unrest. No one has succeeded betting against American's future. That said, no nation in history is forever. No great nation in human history has ever survived the ravages of time. I believe solving the federal debt and global warming problems will severely task American democracy and resilience.

It has been a great honor for me to have been involved in some of the major issues of my time. I have been a player in a number of important issues but have often swum against the tide of conventional thinking. I have had the courage of my convictions, and that, more than any political success, leaves me proud and satisfied as I approach my final years. In 1974, I was selected by *Time Magazine* as one of the two hundred outstanding leaders in America. In 1992, I was honored by the *Denver Post* and Historic Denver, Inc. as one of the "Colorado 100" — people who made significant contributions to Colorado and made lasting impressions on the state's history. I am still in good health and will continue to keep involved in Colorado issues, and the relentless geometry of geometric growth.

ABOUT THE AUTHOR

SKIING, 1986

Richard D. Lamm moved to Colorado in November 1961. Five years later, he was elected to the Colorado state legislature, and in 1975 he was elected governor of Colorado. He was the chief sponsor of the nation's first liberalized abortion bill in 1967, and led the successful fight to reject Denver as the site for the 1976 Winter Olympics. In 1974, he was named one of *Time Magazine*'s "200 Outstanding Young Leaders of America," as well as one of the "Colorado 100" (the 100 people who had the greatest impact on Colorado) by the State Historical Society and the *Denver Post*. Governor Lamm is, by profession, an attorney and a Certified Public Accountant.